Thomas Merton's Dark Path

William H. Shannon

Thomas Merton's Dark Path

THE INNER EXPERIENCE
OF A CONTEMPLATIVE

Farrar · Straus · Giroux

New York

Designed by Dorris J. Huth

Library of Congress Cataloging in Publication Data
Shannon, William Henry
Thomas Merton's dark path.
Bibliography: p.
1. Contemplation—History of doctrines—20th
century.   2. Merton, Thomas, 1915–1968.   I. Title.
BV5091.C7S48   1981   248.3′4   80–28091

Acknowledgements

The author expresses his gratitude for permission to quote material printed by the following publishers:

Reprinted by permission of *American Benedictine Review:* "Thomas Merton 1968: A Profile in Memoriam," by Clifford Stevens, copyright © 1969 by *American Benedictine Review.* Reprinted by permission of Cistercian Publications: *The Climate of Monastic Prayer* by Thomas Merton, copyright © 1969 by the Trustees of the Merton Legacy Trust; *Thomas Merton on St. Bernard,* copyright © 1980 by Cistercian Publications. Reprinted by permission of *Cistercian Studies:* "Merton and the Discovery of the Real Self," by William H. Shannon, copyright © 1978 by *Cistercian Studies.* Reprinted by permission of Doubleday and Co., Inc.: *Conjectures of a Guilty Bystander* by Thomas Merton, copyright © 1965, 1966 by the Abbey of Gethsemani; *Contemplation in a World of Action* by Thomas Merton, copyright © 1965, 1969, 1970, 1971 by the Trustees of the Merton Legacy Trust. Reprinted by permission of Farrar, Straus & Giroux, vi /

Contents

Thomas Merton's Dark Path

Introduction

Thomas Merton was a versatile writer interested in many areas of human concern who felt impelled to write on a wide variety of subjects as his reading, reflection, and dialogue continually expanded the horizons of his interests and concerns. He was a generalist rather than a specialist, his ready pen moving easily from one subject to another. He could write apocalyptic poems about the catastrophic state of world affairs (like the "Original Child Bomb") or a simple poem about a little girl's house ("Grace's House"). He could discourse on the renewal of monastic life in the twentieth century and on the threats of civil strife and international warfare in an age of unrest and social upheaval. He was in no sense a narrow man; and as his reading fed his fertile mind, his writing struck off in many directions. He was an enthusiast who would take up a subject, read all he could find about it, filter it through his rich background, and then offer his readers the fruits of his reading and reflection.

To use an analogy from the photographic art that Merton

was so fond of, he viewed the world through a wide-angle lens, encompassing a wide field of vision. Yet it must be added that frequently, on the camera through which he viewed reality, there was a telephoto lens that focused sharply on a single subject—contemplation. Contemplation was not one of many topics in Merton's field of vision, it was the focal point: the point he frequently and regularly "zoomed in" on. It was the *point vierge* that he speaks of in *Conjectures of a Guilty Bystander,* the center from which his reflections on the human condition came forth and the goal to which they returned. It is no exaggeration to say that contemplation was the explicit theme, or at least the implied background, of everything that Merton wrote. Whatever of import he had to say to his readers is reducible, in ultimate terms, to those things that help or hinder the development of the contemplative dimension of human existence.

Contemplation was the starting point of Merton's anthropology. The story of the fall from paradise in Genesis, which mythologizes the alienation we all experience in our existence, is for Merton the fall from the contemplative state, whereby men and women experience a fragmentation of the human spirit and the loss of their original unity with God and with all that is.

Contemplation is also the key to Merton's understanding of redemption. Redemption is the return to the paradisal state. It is the recovery of the original unity that characterized the human condition as God intended and intends us to be. It is the overcoming of all that alienates us from God, from our own true selves, and from our fellow human beings. The way back to paradise and to original unity is the road of contemplation.

In all his writings, whether he speaks explicitly of contemplation or not, Merton never forgot the primacy of what

Mircea Eliade calls "the eternal return": the return to God and to integral unity, a return effected in this life by contemplation. In his poem "The Captives—A Psalm," which appears in *The Tears of the Blind Lions,* Merton writes:

> May my bones burn and ravens eat my flesh
> If I forget thee, contemplation.

The Tears of the Blind Lions was published in 1949, the year which also saw the publication of *Seeds of Contemplation*—a series of pensées on contemplation that achieved instant popularity. (This was revised in 1962 as *New Seeds of Contemplation.*) A year earlier, Merton had written, at the request of a student at St. Mary's School of Sacred Theology, Notre Dame, a booklet called *What Is Contemplation,* * which was later to be extensively rewritten as *The Inner Experience.* One of his last books, prepared for publication before he left for his trip to the East, but published after his death, was *The Climate of Monastic Prayer,* also published under the title *Contemplative Prayer.* The twenty years that elapsed between the publication of *What Is Contemplation* and *Contemplative Prayer* witnessed an abundance of books and articles that dealt in one way or another with the contemplative experience and more than justify the assertion that Thomas Merton was faithful to the promise he made in his poem, never to forget contemplation.

For Thomas Merton, contemplation was much more than an academic or literary concern; it was a way of life that he strove to live and that he believed all men and women

---

*Sister Madeleva in her autobiography, *My First Seventy Years,* tells of a student who became interested in the poetry of Thomas Merton and wrote to Gethsemani asking for an explanation of contemplation. "His generous answer," Sister Madeleva recounts, "came in manuscript, entitled *What Is Contemplation,* with permission to publish it at St. Mary's if we wished." St. Mary's published the booklet in 1948.

were born for or at least baptized into. In *What Is Contemplation* he links contemplation with baptism. He says that the gifts of the Holy Spirit which make contemplation possible are "part of the normal equipment of Christian sanctity. They are given to all in Baptism, and if they are given, it is presumably because God wants them to be developed." Later in the same work, Merton asserts that the seeds of contemplation

> are planted in every Christian soul at Baptism. But seeds must grow and develop before you reap the harvest. There are thousands of Christians walking about the face of the earth bearing in their bodies the infinite God of whom they know practically nothing. The seeds of contemplation have been planted in these souls, but they merely lie dormant. They do not germinate.

Though in his earlier writings Merton links contemplation with baptism and always remained, in a Christian context, faithful to this intuition, nonetheless, his growing appreciation of Eastern religions, especially Zen, opened his mind to the realization that true contemplation does exist outside the Christian setting. Contemplation, he came to see, was a way of life to which human persons are called in virtue of their humanity. It is not a uniquely Christian phenomenon. Whether the Christian contemplative experience is the same as the Zen satori experience is another matter, and a question that Merton never completely resolved. At times he seems to distinguish them; at other times he seems to identify them as experiences, though his articulation of the Christian experience as a Christian theologian would differ from, say, Suzuki's articulation of the Zen experience as a Zen master. For each would describe the experience in terms consonant with the religious tradition to which he subscribed. But whether the experiences are identical or not and however they are to be described, Merton certainly came to believe that the contemplative experience existed outside the parameters of the Christian community.

Merton believed that the Christian call to contemplation is an invitation extended to all who are willing to undergo the necessary discipline that it requires. Yet he sees the monastic environment as the ideal locus for developing and living the contemplative experience.* For the monastic life is the experience of the desert where one goes to seek God alone and finds sufficiency only in God. This sense of total dependence on God, more easily achieved in a monastic setting, is a necessary prerequisite for contemplation. The monastic life also provides the solitude, without which the contemplative spirit cannot flourish. Merton's own struggle to achieve deeper solitude even in the monastic life indicates the importance he attached to solitude as the atmosphere in which contemplation can flower.

In fact, Merton comes very close to an elitist view of the contemplative life. For while he believed that God manifests himself to all who love him, he seemed to feel that the solitude and discipline essential to contemplation simply could not be achieved "in the world." People who live in the world and unite themselves to God "in the activities of their lives" may very well have an extremely simple prayer life that brings them to the "threshold of contemplation." But it is difficult, if not very nearly impossible, for them to cross that threshold into the realms of true contemplation. Merton describes such persons as "quasi-contemplatives"

---

*This he would hold true not only for Western man but also for Eastern religions. Indeed, it was this conviction—that the monastic traditions of the East had much to offer to Western monks—which prompted his strong desire to meet representatives of Eastern monasticism, especially the Dalai Lama, during his trip to the East.

or "hidden contemplatives."* Their sanctity may well surpass that of the cloistered monk; nonetheless, the doors of contemplation open to them only with the greatest difficulty.†

Merton saw the contemplative experience as an experience of oneness and transcendent unity. The quaint translation of Julian of Norwich puts it this way: "Prayer oneth the soul to God." But first of all it "oneth" the soul to itself. Contemplation brings together the scattered bits of one's person and unifies them in the intuition of the Real Self. This inner unity within oneself makes possible a simultaneous intuition of one's unity with God and with all the creatures he has made. Achieving such unity in the midst of an alienated world calls for much solitude and *ascesis*. Silence and self-discipline, therefore, are necessary preliminaries to opening oneself to the unifying forces that the Spirit of God exercises on the human spirit.

The unity achieved in the contemplative way of life transcends all philosophical and theological systems, even creedal statements, that may attempt to express that unity. To use William James's terms, the experience is a noetic experience that is ineffable. The contemplative "knows," but he cannot articulate, in any satisfactory way, what he knows. "He who knows does not speak; he who speaks, (often) does not know." As Merton puts it:

> The God who in a certain sense is "known" in the articles
> of faith is "known as unknown" beyond those articles. One
> might even say, with some of the Fathers of the Church, that

---

*Merton later adopted a suggestion from Jacques Maritain and referred to such persons as "masked contemplatives" (see *The Inner Experience*, p. 63, third draft).
†"The laity and clergy who are absorbed in many active concerns are unable to give themselves to meditation and to a deeper study of divine and human things (*Contemplation in a World of Action* pp. 182–83).

while our concepts may tell us that "God is," our knowledge of God beyond those concepts is a knowledge of Him "as though He were not," since His being is not accessible to us in direct experience.

Knowing God through concepts (i.e., knowing that "He is") and knowing God beyond concepts (i.e., knowing Him "as though He were not") suggest the two theological traditions that have attempted to express the contemplative experience. The first is the kataphatic tradition; the second, the apophatic tradition.

The kataphatic tradition is the tradition of light; it arrives at an understanding of God through affirmation (the Greek word *kataphasis* means affirmation). We come to know about God by affirming that He possesses all the perfections we find in creatures, though He possesses them to the highest possible degree. Kataphatic articulation of the contemplative experience makes use of symbols drawn from the created order to describe the reality of God. The goodness and beauty of what is finite help us to affirm the goodness and the beauty of what is infinite. Kataphatic theology proceeds by way of analogy. The experiences of fatherhood, of motherhood, of justice, of compassion in a human context—which are our experiences of created being—serve as windows whereby we look out through the created world to the reality of God. These experiences are used analogically to tell us something about God.

But kataphatic theology can only tell us about God or about what He does. It cannot penetrate to His deepest essence, His very life. For no created symbol, however deeply experienced, can adequately mirror the reality of God. That is why there has always been in the Christian mystical tradition a strong apophatic element. Apophaticism is the contemplative tradition of darkness and negation (the Greek word *apophasis* means negation or denial). Apophaticism is an essential step in the truly contemplative experience. For there comes a point in contemplation when concepts and images will no longer do; indeed, they become a hindrance to the deep experience of God. For, while it is true that all creatures bear in themselves the imprint of God, there is, nonetheless, an infinite distance between God and created things. One simply cannot enter through creatures into the presence of God in His own being. Hence, sooner or later, the contemplative must renounce the mind's activity, put out the light of the intellect, and enter into the darkness, wherein there is an "experience" of the ineffable reality of what is beyond experience. The presence of God is "known," not in clear vision, but as "unknown."

The apophatic way has a long history in the Christian mystical tradition. It is the way of Gregory of Nyssa, Pseudo-Dionysius, the author of the *Cloud of Unknowing*, Master Eckhart, John of the Cross, and many others. It is also the way of Thomas Merton. He writes in *Contemplation in a World of Action:*

> The Christian contemplative is aware that in the mystical tradition both of the Eastern and Western Churches there is a strong element of what has been called "apophatic theology." This apophatic tradition concerns itself with the most fundamental datum of all faith—and one which is often forgotten; the God who has revealed Himself to us in His Word has revealed himself as unknown in His ultimate essence, for He is beyond all mere human vision. "You cannot see my face; no man shall see me and live." (Exodus 33:20)

Merton never denied the value of the kataphatic approach to God, but he was strongly convinced that ultimately it must yield place to apophaticism. Thus he writes:

Now, while the Christian contemplative must certainly develop by study, the theological understanding of concepts about God, he is called mainly to penetrate the wordless darkness and apophatic light of an experience beyond concepts, and here he gradually becomes familiar with a God who is "absent" and as it were "non-existent" to all human experience.

Apophaticism thrives on paradoxical expressions. Thus Merton, in the above quotation, speaks of the "wordless darkness" that is "apophatic light." In apophatic contemplation, God is "experienced" as "a dazzling darkness" or as "the brightness of a most lucid darkness." The author of the *Cloud of Unknowing*, who ardently espoused the apophatic way, speaks of two clouds: the cloud of forgetfulness that one must put between himself and creatures (and creatures would include concepts and images) and the cloud of unknowing that one must enter into to find God in a totally ineffable experience. In contemplation, God is known in darkness, i.e., by not knowing Him. God is sought and is found through not finding Him. In a taped lecture given in one of his Sunday sessions with the novices of Gethsemani, Merton quotes Master Eckhart, another enthusiastic exponent of the dark way: "Seek God, so as never to find him." The point Eckhart is making is that, once you seem to have found God, it is not He whom you have found. Once you seem to grasp God, He eludes you. For God is not an object or a thing alongside of other objects and things: God is the All whom we can discover only in the experience of not discovering Him. This is the paradoxical language of the apophatic tradition. It is a way of struggling with words to express that which is beyond all words.

John F. Teahan perceptively points out that the many studies of Merton's works that have been written "have strangely ignored one of the major aspects of his work: his appropriation of the apophatic tradition in Christian mysticism." The thesis of his fine paper is that "Merton's writings exhibit a marked preference for the apophatic tradition. Symbols of darkness and night appear more frequently in his works than symbols of light . . . His enthusiasm for Eastern religions was in part sparked by elements in these traditions that correspond to Christian apophaticism."

A distinctive feature of Merton's apophatic approach to contemplation is his application of the way of darkness and negation to the discovery of our Real Self. His anthropology is as apophatic as his theology. For the Real Self, being our own subjectivity, cannot be known, because it cannot be objectified. For as soon as you attempt to objectify it in images and concepts, you have lost sight of it. You have turned it into an object distinct from subject. The Real Self can only be grasped in an intuitive darkness that coincides in some mysterious way with the intuition of the reality of God.

This book attempts to bring together in summary form what Merton had to say about contemplation. This is a prodigious task, for, as was suggested earlier, contemplation was a central focus and principal thrust of almost everything Merton wrote. The book is intended primarily as a synthesis of Merton's thoughts on contemplation. It is, therefore, expository rather than critical. For the writer is persuaded that a summary presentation of what Merton had to say about contemplation is a useful, and even necessary, prelude to a critical analysis of his theological and anthropological approach to this subject.

The title *Thomas Merton's Dark Path* has been chosen for two reasons. The first is that it highlights Merton's preference for the apophatic tradition; namely, his belief that the dark way of apophaticism is the final path on the contemplative journey. The second reason for the title is that one of the principal motives for writing this book is to acquaint the reader with an important unpublished work of Merton. This book, written in 1959 and called *The Inner Experience,* is an extensive rewrite of Merton's booklet *What Is Contemplation.* Merton's original title for *The Inner Experience* was *The Dark Path.* I have been able to find no explanation as to why he changed the title: but I believe that both the original title and the final one express well the contents of the book. Thus, I have chosen to incorporate them both into the title of this book and have called it *Thomas Merton's Dark Path: The Inner Experience of a Contemplative.*

The contents of this book will present, in chronological order, summary perspectives of Merton's writings on contemplation. Chapter I will discuss his earliest work on the subject, his booklet entitled *What Is Contemplation.* The study of this booklet will be followed by several chapters on what I hope to show are literary "spin-offs" from *What Is Contemplation: Seeds of Contemplation* (1949); *The Ascent to Truth* (1951); and the biggest "spin-off" of all, *The Inner Experience* (1959), the unpublished manuscript mentioned above, which incorporates about ninety percent of the text of *What Is Contemplation.*

The Inner Experience will be studied in two chapters. The first will offer a summary overview of the contents of the manuscript. The second will present selected texts from *The Inner Experience,* so that the most important elements of this work may be made available to Merton scholars and readers. Presently, access to the manuscript is possible only for those who are able to visit the Thomas Merton Studies Center at Bellarmine College in Louisville, Kentucky. The publication of selected passages will be an invaluable service to furthering Merton studies, since some of the most significant things he has to say about contemplation are to be found in this manuscript; and since it will not involve publishing *The Inner Experience* as a book, it will be within the intent of Merton's will expressed in the Trust Agreement.*

The two chapters on *The Inner Experience* will be followed by brief studies of *New Seeds of Contemplation* (1962); *The Climate of Monastic Prayer* (1969), also published under the title *Contemplative Prayer* (1968); and *Zen and the Birds of Appetite* (1968).

The final chapter will attempt to bring together in a brief synthesis some of the basic directions and fundamental perspectives on contemplation discernible in Merton's writings.

This book is written with the conviction that contemporary men and women in large numbers are searching for a greater interiority in their lives. Unhappy with an existence lived merely on the surface of reality, they are increasingly looking inward to their own depths to find purpose and direction in their lives. Such people are ready for the contemplative experience; and Thomas Merton's writings on contemplation can help them move in that direction.

Thomas Merton, it is only fair to say, would be the last person in the world to suggest contemplation as a solution to the problems faced by contemporary men and women. Contemplation, he would say, is not a solution to anything; rather, it is a way of life which may perhaps help you to see that most of the problems you wrestle with are pseudo-problems. For contemplation brings depth to a life that, without it, can only be shallow and superficial. It offers a sense of the authentically Real to a human existence that

---

*The Trust Agreement drawn up by Merton before he left for his trip to the East stipulated that *The Inner Experience* and *The School of the Spirit* were not to be published *as books*.

otherwise would be lived only on the level of the artificial. It introduces an intuition of unity and meaning into human lives that, without the contemplative dimension, are bound to be complex and fragmented.

If you seek contemplation, Merton would tell you, you will probably never find it; but if you dare open your heart to your own inner truth and to God's grace, contemplation may enter your life unobserved. Then, perhaps for the first time, you will know who you are and in knowing yourself you will know God; for it is He, Merton would say, who holds within Himself the secret of your own identity.

I

What Is Contemplation

A small booklet, *What Is Contemplation,* represents Merton's first attempt to put into writing what he had read, studied, and experienced about contemplation in his early years as a monk. Written in 1948,* six or seven years after his entrance into the monastery of Gethsemani, it deals with traditional material on the contemplative life and shows how thoroughly he had absorbed the Western Christian tradition about contemplation. He scarcely breaks new ground on the subject, as he draws his material from the Scriptures, the Fathers of the Church, St. Thomas Aquinas, and writers on the mystical life like his Cistercian Father, St. Bernard of Clairvaux, and especially St. John of the Cross.

---

*This booklet has been reprinted several times. Burns Oates of London published it in 1950, with minor revisions. (The St. Mary's version concluded with a prayer to the Virgin Mary; the Burns Oates edition, being in the *Pater Noster* Series, concluded with a prayer to the Father.) Templegate published the Burns Oates edition in 1951, and again in 1960, in the United States. In 1978, Templegate did another reissue in a different format, with a series of woodcuts, and with the text in seventy-eight small pages.

The booklet is divided into nine sections (numbers added): (1) What Is Contemplation; (2) The Promises of Christ; (3) St. Thomas Aquinas; (4) Kinds of Contemplation; (5) Infused Contemplation; (6) The Test; (7) What to Do; (8) The Danger of Quietism; (9) Prayer. I propose to discuss it in terms of three basic topics that I believe summarize the main content and thrust of the work; namely, the call to contemplation; the two kinds of contemplation; and the three kinds of Christians. The discussion of these three topics will be followed by a brief reflection on the contribution this work makes toward clarifying Merton's understanding of contemplation in his early years in the monastery and also toward indicating directions in which his thought on contemplation might be expected to move.

Merton begins his booklet with a lament that so many Christians have practically no knowledge of God's immense love for them and the power of that love to make them happy. These people do not realize that the gift of contemplation, which is the deepest experience of God's love, is not "something strange and esoteric reserved for a small class of almost unnatural beings and prohibited to everyone else." They do not see that it is the work of the Holy Spirit whose gifts are part of the normal equipment given to all Christians in baptism—gifts that presumably God gives because he wishes them to be developed. Merton's answer, therefore, to the question "Who can desire the gift of infused contemplation?" is: Everyone.

He finds justification for the claim that everyone is called to infused contemplation in the words of Jesus at the Last Supper, in which He promises union with God to the disciples and through them to us. Jesus said that He would send the Holy Spirit to us and that He and the Father would love us and come to abide with us. The abiding presence of God that Jesus promises is in a very true sense an experience of heavenly beatitude on earth. For the knowledge and love of God that comes from the abiding presence of the Trinity within us is "essentially the same beatitude as the blessed enjoy in heaven."

Thus, Merton says, the seeds of perfect union with God —the seeds of contemplation* and sanctity—are planted in every Christian soul at baptism. But it is a sad fact that in thousands of Christians these seeds lie dormant; they never grow. The reason is that so many Christians do not really desire to know God. They are content to remain "surface Christians" whose religious life is largely restricted to external practices. Because they lack any real desire to know God, He will never manifest Himself to them.

Merton quotes St. Thomas Aquinas on the absolute necessity of the desire to know God as a prerequisite for a true life of contemplation. In his commentary on the fourteenth chapter of St. John's Gospel, St. Thomas says: "Spiritualia non accipiuntur nisi desiderata." But he also adds: "nec desiderata nisi aliqualiter cognita." This is to say that there can be no desire for union with God, unless, in some measure at least, one has begun to experience such union. The paradox of the spiritual life is that you cannot know God unless you desire Him, yet at the same time you cannot really desire Him unless, to some degree at least, you have already come to know Him. One cannot have an appetite for a particular food unless he has first tasted it; so one cannot have the desire for God unless he has first in some way tasted the joy of His presence. As Merton puts it: "The only way to find out anything about the joys of contemplation is by experience. We must taste and see that the Lord is sweet."

---

*These words became the title of Merton's next book on the contemplative life, *Seeds of Contemplation.*

How do we acquire a taste for the things of the spirit? The only way is love. Jesus makes it clear that the interior life depends on love, when He says in the discourse at the Last Supper:

> *If you love me . . .* I will ask the Father and He will give you another paraclete . . . *He that loveth me* shall be loved of my Father and *I will love him and manifest myself to him.*

The love Jesus is talking about is not primarily feeling or sentiment; it is love at its deepest level, namely, loving obedience to His word. "If anyone loves me he will keep my word." St. Thomas puts it clearly and simply: "It is obedience that makes a man fit to see God."

Thus, desire based on some experience of love, love feeding desire and leading toward union, together with total uncompromising obedience to the will of Jesus—these are the dispositions needed in order to respond to the invitation, issued at baptism, to achieve union with God in the experience of contemplation.

After discussing the call to contemplation (pp. 3–9), Merton devotes the rest of his booklet (pp. 9–25) to an explanation of what contemplation is. He makes it clear that there is only one kind of contemplation in its strict and correct sense; namely, infused or pure or passive contemplation. This is a gift of God that we simply cannot achieve by our own efforts; it is a pure gift of God that involves a direct and experimental contact with God as He is in himself. It means emptying oneself of every created love to be filled with the love of God. It means going beyond all created images to receive the simple light of God's substantial presence.

There is a second type of prayer, analogous to infused contemplation, which Merton, following the tradition of Western mystical literature, calls active contemplation. Active contemplation, which is something that anyone can achieve by cooperating with God's ordinary grace, means a number of things to Merton. It is not restricted to a particular exercise or a single type of experience. It includes the use of reason, imagination, and the affections of the will. It draws on the resources of theology, philosophy, art, and music. It may involve vocal prayer, meditation, or affective prayer. It introduces a person to the joys of the interior life, showing him how to seek God in His will and how to be attentive to His presence. It builds in him the desire to please God rather than to enjoy the satisfactions of the world. It leads toward love and toward union with God in love.

The highest expression of active contemplation is the liturgy, which, with its rich fare of scripture, theology, music, art, and poetry, teaches one to be contemplative. Indeed, it may become the point of transition from active to passive contemplation. For, in the liturgy, Christ draws us to Himself. But Christ is, quite literally, the "embodiment" of contemplation, since His humanity is perfectly united to the Godhead. Hence, by drawing us to Himself, inevitably He draws us toward union with the Godhead and, therefore, toward infused contemplation.*

What makes active contemplation similar to infused contemplation is that the goal of both is union with God in love. What differentiates the two is that active contemplation is union with God in the liturgy of the Church or in the activities of one's life, whereas infused contemplation is union with God as He is in Himself. One way, perhaps, of expressing Merton's thought is to distinguish the immanence of God from His transcendence. The immanence of

---

*Liturgy may, not infrequently, be the occasion for moments of intuition akin to infused contemplation, especially when the appropriate periods of silence are observed in the liturgy.

God is His presence in all reality; the transcendence of God is His very Being, as He is in Himself. In infused contemplation, one experiences both; in active contemplation, one ordinarily experiences only the first.

Infused contemplation, therefore, because it involves experiencing God as He is in Himself, is contemplation in the strictest sense of the terms, while active contemplation deserves the name of contemplation only by way of analogy. It must be pointed out, however, that the experience of the immanence of God in active contemplation can lead to a very deep love of God. Indeed, it could happen, in particular situations, that active contemplation could generate a deeper love of God than that achieved by some who may be pure contemplatives. "Such Christians as these," Merton says of those who live lives of active contemplation, "far from being excluded from perfection, may reach a higher degree of sanctity than others who have been apparently favored with a deeper interior life." Infused contemplation, while it is the experience of God at a deeper level, does not necessarily mean a deeper love for God than that which can be achieved in active contemplation.

It would seem correct to say that, in speaking of the interior life, Merton would distinguish three types of "practicing" Christians, namely (1) those who obey God but do not really love Him ("surface Christians"); (2) those who love God and are united with Him in the activities of their lives ("quasi-contemplatives");* (3) those who love God

---

*By "quasi-contemplatives" Merton appears to mean those whose interior lives involve active contemplation. Nowhere, however, does he speak of "active contemplatives." This may be because he considered such a term inappropriate and misleading, holding as he did that there is only one kind of contemplation in the strict sense of the term. In *The Inner Experience*, Merton drops the term "quasi-contemplative" and speaks of "hidden" or "masked" contemplatives. The latter term he got from Jacques Maritain, to whom on February 10, 1949, he wrote: "Thank you for your kind remarks on *What Is Contemplation* and I especially like

and experience Him as He is in Himself (pure contemplatives).

First of all, there are the "surface Christians," whose interior life, if indeed it may be called that at all, is "confined to a few routine exercises of piety and a few external acts of worship and service performed as a matter of duty." Their predominant symbol of God is that of One who rewards and punishes. They seek not Him but His rewards. Their spiritual goal in life is to achieve heaven and to avoid hell. They respect God as a Master; but their hearts belong not to Him, but to their own ambitions, cares, and concerns. They are not contemplative in any sense of the word; in no way do they taste the joys of union with God. They have no thought of seeking His presence. They willfully remain at a distance from Him. They live lives of divided allegiance, allowing God to maintain His rights over the substance of their souls, but with their thoughts and desires turned not toward Him but toward the world and external things. As far as experiencing God is concerned, they are in the same condition as men and women who refuse to acknowledge God at all.

Very different from "surface Christians" are those whom Merton describes as "quasi-contemplatives." These are Christians who truly love God and are united with Him in the activities of their lives. They serve God "with great purity of heart and perfect self-sacrifice in the active life." Their vocation to the active life does not allow them the

---

the term 'masked contemplatives,' which expresses better what I mean. As far as I know they *are* contemplatives, but they have no way of really knowing what they are because their gifts of understanding and wisdom are not strong enough to enable them to recognize their experience for what it is. They know God by experience, but they can't interpret the experience. (There must be very many like that even here, and I think they sometimes get upset at the thought that they ought to be mystics and they are afraid that they are not.)"

solitude and silence required for a life of infused contemplation; nor do their temperaments suit them for such a life. They would probably be uncomfortable if they gave up all activity for a life of solitude.

This does not mean that they cannot live interior lives or that the only alternative for them is a life of "surface Christianity." On the contrary, the promise of Christ that the three divine Persons will manifest themselves to all who love them is meant for them as well as for pure contemplatives. Though they may not be able to empty themselves of created things to lose themselves in God alone, as the pure contemplative tries to do, still they serve God with great purity of heart, expressed in fraternal charity, self-sacrifice, and total abandonment to God's will in all that they do and suffer. They serve God in His children on earth. They learn to find Him in their activities, living and working in His company, remaining in His presence and tasting the deep peaceful joy of that presence.

Their prayer life may be very ordinary, not rising above the level of vocal and affective prayer. Yet, because they are conscious of God's presence, their humble prayer may result in a deep interior life that brings them to the threshold of contemplation. Hence, though they are living active lives in the world, they may be called "quasi-contemplatives." They are not unfamiliar with graces akin to contemplation. Indeed, they may experience moments of true contemplation in their simple prayer life, in the liturgy, in the consciousness of God's presence in their lives as they go about fulfilling their daily responsibilities. They have fleeting moments, perhaps sometimes even prolonged periods of time, in which their intuition of oneness with God becomes a very vivid experience. Because of this union with God, immanent in their lives' activities, they may achieve a high degree of sanctity—even, perhaps, higher than that of some who may have a genuine vocation to infused contemplation.

Besides the "surface Christians" and the "quasi-contemplatives," there is a third group of Christians who may be called pure contemplatives. It is about them and for them that *What Is Contemplation* is especially written. These pure contemplatives, who, Merton believes, will always be a small minority in the Christian community, are the people of the "desert," whose sole goal in life is to search for God and who find their sufficiency in Him alone. They live lives of solitude and silence in which they can empty themselves of all things outside of God, so that their emptiness can be filled with His transcendent presence. They alone are contemplatives in the strict sense. Merton writes: "In the strict sense of the word, contemplation is a supernatural Love and Knowledge of God, simple and obscure, infused by Him into the summit of the soul, giving it a direct and experimental contact with Him as He is in Himself."

Following the tradition of the Fathers of the Church, Merton stresses the purity of love that is at the heart of true contemplation. It is pure in that it empties the soul of all affection for things that are not God. It is pure in that it desires no reward, not even the reward of contemplation. This is to say that the reward of pure love is not something outside of love itself; it is simply the ability to love. In the words of St. Bernard of Clairvaux: "I love simply because I love and I love in order to love." Amo quia amo, amo ut amem (Serm. 83 in Cantica).

This disinterested love of God always brings peace and strength to the soul. Yet it would be a mistake to think "that infused contemplation is all sweetness and understanding and consolation and joy." There are times when the peace it brings is almost buried under pain and darkness and aridity. There are times when the strength it gives seems to be shrouded in an extreme sense of helplessness and incapacity.

The reasons for this darkness and helplessness are to be found in the very nature of the contemplative experience. For contemplation is the Light of God shining directly on the soul. But because the soul is weakened by Original Sin, the Light of God affects the soul the way the light of the sun affects a diseased eye. It causes pain. The soul, diseased by its own selfishness, is shocked and repelled by the purity of God's light. The brightness of this Light shatters the ideas of God that one has formed by his own reason. God as He is in Himself is not the God we imagined Him to be. It also shatters the ideas one has formed of himself; the flame of the divine light attacks a person's self-love and he no longer knows who he is before God.

Thus, "infused contemplation sooner or later brings with it a terrible revolution." The God we thought we had known is taken away from us and the mind is no longer able to think of Him. The joy of His presence is gone, because we no longer know Him who is present. We are not even sure that Anyone is present at all. The will that once loved God so ardently seems unable to love, because the object of love seems to have disappeared into impenetrable darkness. We no longer have Anyone even to pray to; hence, "gone is the sweetness of prayer. Meditation becomes impossible, even hateful." Liturgy turns into a boring exercise that appears to be without meaning. The ray of light becomes, for a time at least, "a ray of darkness": it seems to remove everything we have known and loved, while leaving nothing in its place. One experiences the deep meaning of St. John's words: "The light shineth in the darkness and the darkness did not comprehend it" (John 1:5).

This is a crucial point in the life of prayer. For a person

wants to depend on himself and make his own decisions, yet he finds himself called to wait for God to act. A person wants to know where he is going, yet he finds himself called to walk in emptiness with blind trust. A person wants to know at least that he is on the right path, yet he finds himself in a darkness that seems to deprive him of the certainty he once thought he had about God and about himself.

How can he know that he is on the right path, especially when he sees no path at all? How can he know whether this pain of separation from the God he once thought he knew is a real separation from God or the experience of a darkness wherein the true God is met more fully and deeply? How does he know whether what is happening to him is the beginning of infused contemplation or simply a growing distaste for the interior life that may signal an eventual return to a Christian life that is devoted largely to externals?

There are no easy answers to these questions; but the surest test that infused contemplation is beginning behind this cloud of darkness is "a powerful, mysterious and yet simple attraction which holds the soul prisoner in this darkness and obscurity." Although frustration is experienced, there is no desire to escape from the darkness and return to an easier stage of the spiritual life that preceded entrance into the darkness. At the same time, "there is a growing conviction that joy and peace and fulfillment are only to be found somewhere in this night of aridity and faith."

Then one day there is an illumination. The soul comes to realize that in this darkness it has truly found the living God. It is overwhelmed with the sense that He is present and that His love surrounds the soul on all sides and absorbs it. The darkness does not cease to be darkness, but, by the strangest of all paradoxes, it has become brighter than the brightest day. Life is transformed and there is only one thought and one love: GOD ALONE. The soul has been awakened. It has entered on what writers on the mystical life have called the illuminative way. Truly awakened to the reality of God, it is being drawn toward union with Him as He is in Himself.

How does one deal with this new experience? this awakening? this call to move from illumination to union with God? For help in answering this critical question, Merton turns to the writings of the great sixteenth-century Spanish mystic, St. John of the Cross. Drawing on *The Dark Night, The Ascent of Mount Carmel,* and *The Spiritual Canticle,* Merton offers several guidelines to help the awakened soul on the path toward contemplative union with God. These guidelines may be summarized as follows:*

1. First of all, it is important that you know what God is doing in your soul and accept it. His purpose is to bring you to "the threshold of an actual experimental contact with the living God." John of the Cross says that in this Dark Night

> God secretly teaches the soul and instructs it in the perfection of love without its doing anything or understanding of what manner is this infused contemplation. (*Dark Night* II, v, 1)

If you realize what God is doing, you will not seek the very things God is trying to drive out of you; namely, the precise concepts you have had of Him and the sweetness and consolation you have experienced in prayer. You must know when to leave meditation and affections behind. God wants to replace these created experiences with His presence: He

---

*The numbers are the writer's, not Merton's.

wants to infuse into your soul His Light (to replace your concepts of Him) and His Love (to replace the consolations and sweetness you had heretofore been experiencing in prayer). Let God act! If you attempt by your own action to increase the precision of your knowledge of God or to intensify your feeling of love, you will interfere with His work.

2. Find solitude as much as you can. Live as much as possible in peace, quiet, and retirement. Do the tasks appointed to you as perfectly as you can with disinterested love, wanting only to please God. Do not strive for spectacular "experiences," such as you read about in the lives of the great mystics.

> None of these graces (called *gratis datae*) can sanctify you nearly as well as this obscure and purifying light and love of God which is given you to no other end than to make you perfect in His love.

3. Do not be overanxious about your progress in prayer. "You have left the beaten track and are travelling by paths that cannot be chartered or measured." Let God take care of your prayer and your progress in it. Seek only to purify your love of God more and more. Seek only to abandon yourself more and more perfectly to His will.

4. Accept the trials and crosses that God sends you, even though they baffle you. Know that God is using them to form his image in you more and more perfectly.

5. Above all, realize that sanctity and pure contemplation are only to be found in the perfection of love.

> The truly contemplative soul is not one that has the most exalted visions of the Divine Essence but the one who is most closely united to God in the purity of love and allows itself to be absorbed and transformed into Him by that love.

Let everything, pleasant or unpleasant, be a source and occasion of love. Merton quotes the celebrated passage from the *Spiritual Canticle* on the bee.

> Even as the bee extracts from all plants the honey that is in them and has no use for them for aught else save for that purpose, *even so the soul with great facility extracts the sweetness of love that is in all things that pass through it.* IT LOVES GOD IN EACH OF THEM, WHETHER PLEASANT OR UNPLEASANT.
>
> (*Spiritual Canticle* xxvii)

Such love leads to a holy indifference, the *apatheia* that the Fathers of the Church speak of, wherein the only thing that matters is to please the Beloved.

Merton concludes his "borrowings" from St. John of the Cross with a quotation from the *Spiritual Canticle* on the value of contemplation:

> Let those that are great actives and think to girdle the world with their outward works take note that *they would bring far more profit to the Church and be far more pleasing to God if they spent even half this time in abiding with God in prayer* . . . Of a surety they would accomplish more with one piece of work than they now do with a thousand and that with far less labor. (*Spiritual Canticle* xxix, 3)

What Is Contemplation leaves a number of questions unanswered, especially questions about the call to contemplation and the distinction between infused contemplation and active contemplation.

In the introduction Merton openly and with enthusiasm espouses the egalitarian view that all are called to contemplation. For all are given in baptism the gifts of the Holy Spirit that are intended by God to produce as their fruit the life of contemplation. "Why," Merton asks, "do we think of contemplation, infused contemplation, mystical prayer as something essentially strange and esoteric reserved for a small class of almost unnatural beings and prohibited to everyone else?"

Yet further on he moves full-circle to an elitist view of contemplation: he states quite clearly that few will achieve it. "The great majority of Christians," he says, "will never become pure contemplatives on earth."

The discrepancy between these two perspectives he seems to resolve initially in terms of the desire for contemplation. He writes: "God often measures His gifts by our desire to receive them." This would seem to mean that the reason the majority of Christians never become pure contemplatives is that they lack the desire.

Yet later Merton appears to reduce the difference between pure contemplatives and "quasi-contemplatives," not to desire or its lack, but to a difference in life style. Pure contemplatives have the silence and solitude necessary for the true contemplative experience; "quasi-contemplatives" do not. Merton admits that the latter, because of purity of heart, "maintained by obedience, fraternal charity, self-sacrifice and perfect abandonment to God's will, may well achieve a greater sanctity than those who have been apparently favored with a deeper interior life." Certainly, therefore, these "quasi-contemplatives" have a desire for union with God. It would appear, therefore, that life style, rather than desire, is the practical determinant as to whether or not they can respond to the call to contemplation as a way of union with God.

If this is a correct reading of Merton's thought, it means that he is really saying that the call to infused contemplation, given theoretically to all, can in practice be responded to only in the monastic life or at most in a life style that reproduces the solitude and silence that characterize the monastic life.

While this interpretation of Merton's thought severely

limits the eligibility list for infused contemplation, it is not intended in any way to suggest that Merton saw the monastery as the only breeding ground for sanctity. Merton certainly believed that sanctity is something that all men and women can achieve, whatever their state in life. For sanctity is primarily a matter of love.

Would Merton, perhaps, have been better advised to suggest that the call to sanctity, rather than the call to infused contemplation, is given to all, but that infused contemplation as a way to sanctity is restricted to the few? Would it have been enough for him to say that infused contemplation is a special and unique way to sanctity, but that there is also another way: the way of active contemplation?

Yet, answering these questions in the affirmative would still leave unanswered a whole other series of questions:

1. Does union with God as He is in Himself (which is the goal of pure contemplation) produce of itself greater sanctity than union with God in the activities of one's life (which would ordinarily be the highest achievement possible to the "quasi-contemplative")?

2. How does union with God in His transcendent Being differ from union with God in the activities of one's life?

3. What does it mean to be united to God in the activities of one's life?

4. Can a person be united with God in the activities of his life without, in some measure at least, being united with God as He is in Himself?

5. Does the pure contemplative differ from the "quasi-contemplative," not in the sense that his union with God is different from that of the "quasi-contemplative," but simply in the sense that his experience of that union is different?

These questions, suggested but left unanswered by *What*

Is Contemplation, may well be kept in mind, as we venture further into Merton's writings on the contemplative life.

One thing concerning *What Is Contemplation* about which there can be no question is Merton's appropriation of the "apophatic way," the way of night and darkness, as his preferred approach to describing the contemplative experience. He speaks of "the curtain of darkness," "the cloud of obscurity," "the cloud of darkness," "the night of aridity and faith," "the night of faith," "the power of an obscure love," "the ray of darkness."

Yet it is important to realize that for Merton the darkness of the apophatic way must be understood dialectically. It is one way of expressing the experience, but it never conveys the total experience. Thus it is darkness from our side (because the light of our faculties is put out), but not from God's side (for it is the very intensity of His light that causes the darkness). The darkness of the apophatic way is never complete and total darkness. That is why Merton speaks of the *power* of an obscure love. That is why he speaks of the *ray* of darkness, which is really a ray of light but so brilliant a light that it blinds us so as to leave room for the activity of God. That is why the love that is obscure is yet a love that has *power.* That is why the "ray of darkness" is still a *ray.* "The darkness remains as dark as ever and yet, somehow, it seems to have become brighter than the brightest day."

Merton's apophaticism will be developed in more detail in the discussion of his later works. This work sufficiently establishes him in the apophatic tradition.

II

Seeds of Contemplation

Seeds of Contemplation, published in 1949, became almost immediately a very popular book. After it went through several printings, a revised edition was published in December 1949. This revised edition is to be distinguished from *New Seeds of Contemplation,* which was published in 1962 and represents a far more extensive revision than that of December 1949.*

Seeds of Contemplation derives its title from a passage in Merton's earlier work, *What Is Contemplation:*

> The seeds of this perfect life (i.e., the life of contemplative union with God) are planted in every Christian soul in Baptism. But seeds must grow before you reap the harvest. There are thousands of Christians walking about the face of the earth bearing in their bodies the infinite God of Whom they know practically nothing.

---

*Merton said of *New Seeds:* "It is in many ways a completely new book" (*New Seeds of Contemplation,* p. ix). See Donald Grayston, "Nova in Novibus: The New Material in Thomas Merton's *New Seeds of Contemplation.*"

The seeds of contemplation and sanctity are planted in these souls, but (in so many cases) they merely lie dormant.

Seeds of Contemplation is an invitation to those thousands of Christians to bring these seeds to fruition and harvest.

The book is not a formal or systematic study of the contemplative experience. Merton describes it as "a collection of notes and personal reflections." It is a series of pensées, some developed to lead the reader to deeper understanding, others given and then quickly dropped to allow the reader to ponder their meaning on his own. It is a poetic reflection on contemplation, full of intuitions and insights. It is the work of a poet creating a book and at the same time, one feels, being created as a contemplative by God. "The poet," Merton writes, "enters into himself to create. The contemplative enters into God to be created." Both these facets of Merton's personality—the poetic and the contemplative—are at work in this book. The book has a freshness and creativity about it that produces moments of sheer poetry, like, for example, his description of the poverty and emptiness of contemplation:

> We are like vessels empty of water that they may be filled with wine. We are like glass cleansed of dust and grime to receive the sun and vanish into its light.

The book also suggests that Merton is writing about what he has come to know through experience. The words of the introduction have the ring of autobiography about them:

> By receiving His will with joy and doing it with gladness, I have His love in my heart, because my will is now the same as His Love and I am on the way to become what He is, Who is Love.

Seeds of Contemplation is a very different book from *What Is Contemplation.* The latter could have come from the pen of a man of poetic bent who had *studied* contemplation. *Seeds* comes from a poet who has *tasted* the joys of contemplation—a poet who could enter into himself and create a moving book on contemplation, because he had already entered into God and allowed himself to be created as a contemplative.

In writing about contemplation Merton, here as elsewhere, struggles with the paradox of the gratuity of the contemplative experience and yet, at the same time, its naturalness. It "utterly transcends everything [we] are and can ever be." It raises us "above our natural capacity"; yet at the same time it is the very reason for our existence. In *What Is Contemplation,* Merton sees contemplation as the reason why we were baptized: it is the fruition of the gratuitous gifts of the Spirit offered to us in our baptism. In *Seeds,* without sacrificing the supernatural character of contemplation, Merton has a deeper perception: he sees contemplation as "the only real reason why [we] were created."

> Contemplation by which we know and love God as He is in Himself, apprehending Him in a deep and vital experience which is beyond the reach of human understanding, is the *reason* for our creation by God.

The ever-present paradox of contemplation that Merton consistently highlights is that, while it is above our nature, it is yet "the fulfillment of deep capacities in us." The life of heaven *is* a life of contemplation. "All those who reach the end for which they were created will therefore be contemplatives in heaven." But we do not have to wait for heaven. The goal of contemplation can be achieved in this life—and not just by the few. "Many," Merton says, "are also destined to enter this supernatural element and breathe this new atmosphere while they are still on earth." And it was to broadcast this message that Merton wrote his book. As he says in the Author's Note at the beginning of the book: "[The book] has no other end or ideal in view than what should be the ordinary fulfillment of the Christian life and therefore everything that is said here can be applied to anyone, not only in the monastery, but also in the world."

The reader will note that this is a backing away from the more rigid position adopted by Merton in *What Is Contemplation,* where he said: "The great majority of Christians will never become pure contemplatives on earth." Now he is saying that many are destined to become contemplatives while still on earth. It is possible to reconcile these statements by suggesting that when Merton speaks of "many" being destined for contemplation, he has in mind what in the earlier book he called active contemplation, and not infused or pure contemplation. Yet this distinction, so carefully drawn in *What Is Contemplation,* does not appear in *Seeds.* * What Merton seems to be talking about throughout *Seeds* is what he called, in the earlier book, infused or pure contemplation. It would seem fair, therefore, to say that in *Seeds* Merton has modified his earlier position: contemplation is not restricted to the few; many are destined to achieve its joys in this life.

What is this experience of contemplation that is at once beyond our natural powers and yet also a fulfillment of deep capacities that God has put in us? As was indicated earlier, *Seeds* gives no systematic answer to this question. Contemplation is presented in a variety of ways: it is a precious jewel with many facets that Merton keeps turning in many directions to help us see different aspects of this rich and enriching experience. I propose in this chapter to

---

*Merton speaks in *Seeds* about the activity of the contemplative, but not about active contemplation.

discuss *Seeds* in terms of three unifying themes that seem to thread their way through the book: (1) contemplation as Discovery: the discovery of the True God, the discovery of the True Self, the discovery of other persons; (2) contemplation as an experience of freedom; and (3) contemplation as an experience of darkness.

SEED OF GOD.* Contemplation is a discovery of my dependence on God and the implications of that dependence. "There exists," Merton says, "some point at which I can meet God in a real and experimental contact with His infinite actuality: and it is the point where my contingent being depends upon His Love."

The "point" Merton speaks of is a point of mysterious identity that is neither a created reality nor an uncreated reality but a "place" where both intersect. It is a point where, in a mystery beyond fathoming, God and I are one and I experience Him.

The secret, of course, is that I must really *meet* Him at this point. If I do not really meet *Him,* the God on whom I think I depend will be a fictitious God of my own making; and I will not meet him. Indeed, I cannot meet him because such a God does not exist. He is an idol.

But if I really meet *Him* at this point of intersection of what is divine and what is human, the One I meet will be the True God as He is in Himself. For the God on Whom I actually depend can only be the True God as He is in His own reality. Nothing less than the True God can be the One on Whose Love I depend for my very existence.

My discovery of my dependence on God is in a way also His "discovery" of my dependence on Him. God "discov-

---

*The first epistle of John (3:9) speaks of the human person as the *sperma theou,* the "seed of God."

ers" me as dependent on Him the moment I begin to exist. He sees me in Himself and Himself in me. He "lives in me, not only as my creator, but as my other and true self." He discovers me in that pure contemplation that is His own infinite actuality. And I, being in Him, swim in a sea of contemplation. As Merton puts it: "We become contemplatives when God discovers Himself in us." Since God's "discovery" of us coincides with our coming into being, it is true to say that we do not really become contemplatives. In a sense we already are contemplatives, because we exist in Him who is pure contemplation. The problem is that we do not realize that we are contemplatives because we do not actualize our capacity. But the capacity is there, inherent in our dependence on Him. But when we truly *meet Him* at that point of dependence, it is a real and experimental contact with His infinite actuality. We become at the center of our being the contemplatives we were always meant to be.

Because we are contemplatives in the very center of our being, the contemplative experience, when finally we reach it, is never a complete surprise to us. As Merton says: when we first taste the joys of contemplation, "it strikes us at once as utterly new and strangely familiar." "Although we had an entirely different notion of what it would be like, it turns out to be just what you seem to have known all along that it ought to be." "We enter into a region which we had never even suspected, and yet it is this new world which seems familiar and obvious." In contemplation we return to a place where we have never been.

SEEDS OF MY OWN IDENTITY.* Contemplation is not only the discovery of the True God at my center; it is also the discovery at the same center of my True Self. For "the only

---

*"The seeds planted in my liberty are the seeds of my own identity" (p. 27).

way I can be myself is to become identified with Him in Whom is hidden the reason and fulfillment of my existence." God's love and mercy are the reason for my existence.* His peace is the fulfillment of my existence.

> Since God alone possesses the secret of my identity, He alone can make me who I am or, rather, He alone can make me who I will be when I at last fully begin to be.

For He bears in Himself "the secret of who I am." I find my true self by finding Him or, what amounts to the same thing, I "discover who I am and possess my true identity by losing myself in Him."

Just as the God whom I discover at my center is not a false god, not an idol I have constructed by my imagination, but the True God as He is in Himself, so the self I discover in God cannot be the false self I have constructed by my own desires and ambitions; it must be my True Self. I cannot live with an illusion of myself any more than I can live with an illusion of God.

That is why, before I can become who I am meant to be, I must recognize that I am "shadowed by an illusory person, a false self." My false self exists, but at the level of illusion; it has no ultimate reality. It is the self I imagine I am, not the self that I am at my center. The great tragedy of human life is to go through it living as a self that I am not. This is what it means to experience the effects of Original Sin. Original Sin, whose effects survive baptism, is a habitual state in which my acts tend to keep alive "the illusion that is opposed to God's reality in me." It is, there-

---

*"The secret of my identity is hidden in the *love and mercy* of God" (p. 29). "To say that I am made in the image of God is to say that *love* is the reason for my existence: for God is love" (p. 46). "Our life becomes a series of choices between the fiction of our false-self . . . and our true identity in the *peace* of God" (pp. 33–34).

fore, the myth of Original Sin that begets the myth of the false self.*

In fact, all sin, original or personal, starts from the assumption that my false self is "the fundamental reality of life." I feed this illusion by self-seeking and self-aggrandizement. I construct the nothingness of the false self into what appears to be real. My life becomes an accumulation of accidents (in the Aristotelian sense) without substance.

> I am hollow and my structure of pleasures and ambitions has no foundation. I am objectified in them. But they are destined by their very contingency to be destroyed. And when they are gone, there will be nothing left of me but my own nakedness and emptiness and hollowness, to tell me that I am a mistake.

When Merton speaks of sin, he has in mind, not primarily a moral lapse whereby I choose what is in conflict with my better instincts, but an ontological lapse whereby I choose what is in conflict with my true being. It is not simply that I make mistakes. I become a mistake. For I become what I am not.

But the mistake can be overcome, I can choose to drop the mask, the illusion, of my false self and achieve my true identity in God. Indeed, from the moment I become capable of conscious acts of love, "[my] life becomes a series of choices between the fiction of [my] false self whom [I] feed with the illusion of passion and selfish appetite and [my] true identity in the peace of God."

Only God can teach me to make the right choices. He teaches me when I meet Him at the center of my being; at the point of my dependence on Him. That is why I must

---

*Myth is used here not as a false notion but as an intuition that gives insight into the condition of human existence.

learn to "draw all the powers of my soul down into its deepest center to rest in silent expectancy for the coming of God, poised in tranquil and effortless concentration upon the point of my dependence on Him." That is why the journey to my true identity is a journey along the way to contemplation. On that journey I learn to give up my false self, so that I can find my identity in God. And at the culmination of the journey "God identifies a created life with his own life, so that there is nothing left of any significance but God living in God."*

Contemplation is an experience in solitude, but it is not an experience in isolation. My contemplation leads me not only to God but also to other human persons. The point of dependence where I meet God is the same point at which I meet others, for they are no less dependent on God than I. Meeting others, then, is an aspect of discovering my own identity, because I was never intended to exist in separateness. "I must look for my identity somehow not only in God but in other men."

> The more I become identified with God (at my center), the more will I be identified with others who are identified with Him. His Spirit will live in all of us. We shall love one another and God with the same love with which He loves us and Himself.

A contemplative must at some time go into the desert, but he must not go there to escape others, but in order to find them in God. It is dangerous to seek solitude "merely because you happen to like to be alone."

In His discourse at the Last Supper, Christ prayed that all might become one with the oneness that He has with the

---

*See also p. 198: "So it is with one who has vanished into God by pure contemplation. God alone is left. He is the only identity that acts there. He is the only one Who loves and knows and rejoices."

Father in the Holy Spirit. When we achieve our true identity and become what God really intends us to be, we will discover that we love one another perfectly and that we all form the One Mystical Person that is Christ living in us.

There is something incomplete about contemplation if it is not shared. That is why heaven, where the ultimate perfection of contemplation will be achieved, will not be a place of separate individuals, each with his own private vision of God; rather, it will be a sea of Love flowing through the One Person of all the elect.

This sea of love in which we find our oneness with all is the life of the Three Persons of God. In God there is no selfishness or isolation.

> The three selves of God are Three Subsistent Relations of selflessness overflowing and superabounding in joy in the perfection of their gift of their One Life to One Another.

This "circulation of love" in God "never finds a Self that is capable of halting and absorbing it, but only another principle of communication and return." This Love of the Three Persons is contemplation. Our joy and our destiny are to participate in this Love, so that we can live entirely in and for God and one another.

Contemplation in this life is meant to reflect its heavenly counterpart. Even here on earth, "the more we are alone with God, the more we are united with one another and the silence of contemplation is [a] deep and rich and endless society, not only with God but with men."

And yet our efforts to achieve union with others in Christ is always a struggle. What is experienced with clarity in heaven is experienced only in obscurity in this life. For in heaven our thoughts of others can only draw us closer to God, whereas on earth, if we turn our thoughts directly to others in prayer, we may be distracted by their separateness and so be withdrawn from union with God and likewise from union with them.

In heaven we meet others in the bright clarity of the purest contemplative vision; on earth we most often find them and God in a contemplation that is dark and obscure. But for the present it is in this darkness that we must try to find ourselves and others as we all truly are. The darkness becomes for us a sea of Love, if not Light, in which at last we become real and know that reality is to be found not in separateness but in union.

The seeds of contemplation that God plants in us can grow and develop only in the context of freedom. For they are seeds "planted in my liberty." If I am to actualize my capacity for contemplation, then, I must become a free person. And Merton has much to say about what it means to be a free person.

Perhaps the most important aspect of freedom, which in a sense encompasses its whole meaning, is the freedom to see things as they really are. This is the freedom that liberates me from anything that would tend "in one way or another to keep alive in me the illusion that is opposed to God's reality living in me." This illusion is my false self. As long as I perceive no greater subjective reality in me than my false self, I have no freedom. I cannot seek God. I cannot become contemplative. My illusory self may talk about contemplation, even try to become contemplative; but it can never succeed, for the subject of contemplation can only be a self that really exists. The shadow of the self cannot be contemplative any more than the shadow of a tree can produce fruit.

To have this freedom to see things as they are, I must also be free from selfishness, that is to say, from the desires and attachments that feed the false self. I must not use up my life accumulating pleasures and experiences and power and honors that clothe my false self and attempt to construct its essential nothingness into something objectively real. I must escape "from the prison of my own selfhood" so as to "enter by love into union with the Life that dwells and sings within the essence of every creature and in the core of our own souls."

Until I have managed this escape, I will not be seeing things as they really are. Indeed, the very things that God has created to attract me to Himself will keep me away from Him. For I will linger on them, making them the objects of my self-seeking, instead of letting them lead me to God. It is only when I am delivered from self-seeking that I am free to seek God and nothing else. Freedom means, therefore, the complete destruction in me of all selfishness.

It is easier to speak about deliverance from selfishness than to achieve it. For selfishness is an elusive "reality" that at times I can identify only with great difficulty. For selfishness may mean something going on in my life that I am conscious of; but it may also mean something happening in me of which I am almost totally unaware. In other words, there may be obvious attachments in my life that deter me from seeking God, and because they are obvious, I can really recognize them and, hopefully, deal with them. But there may also be attachments that are not so obvious: hidden and subtle attachments that I am unaware of and therefore not really able to deal with. For example, a contemplative may think that he is seeking God in his prayer when in reality he is seeking the consolations that God sometimes gives with prayer: recollection, interior peace, and the sense of His presence. Clinging to these spiritual experiences can be, even if ever so unconsciously, an attachment to creatures that prevents us from truly seeking God and therefore that blocks the way to true contemplation.

> Recollection is just as much a creature as an automobile. The sense of interior peace is no less a creature than a bottle of wine. The experimental "awareness" of the presence of God is just as truly a created thing as a glass of beer.

Selfishness can hide itself under many guises. I need the discernment to uncover its presence and its different forms. For until I am fully conscious that it is there I can do nothing to free myself from it.

What would it be like to be totally free? In a moving passage Merton offers a portrait of a person of perfect freedom in words intended, one hopes, not to discourage the reader but to show how deep is the reality of freedom and how rare its perfect achievement.

> I wonder if there are twenty men alive in the world now who see things as they really are. That would mean that there were twenty men who were free, who were not dominated or even influenced by any attachment to any created thing or to their own selves or to any gift of God, even the highest, the most supernaturally pure of His graces. I don't believe that there are twenty such men alive in the world. But there must be one or two. They are the ones who are holding everything together and keeping the universe from falling apart.

The path to perfect freedom is a difficult one. For Merton it must always lead into the desert; that is, into the place of silence and solitude.* Only in solitude can we come to see things as they are. Only in solitude can we achieve that detachment that frees us to seek God in our lives. That is why Merton always saw the monastic setting as the ideal locus for contemplation. ". . . Physical solitude, exterior silence and real recollection are all morally necessary for anyone who wants to lead a contemplative life."

Can one find sufficient solitude to become a contempla-

---

*"The ordinary way to contemplation lies through a desert . . ." (p. 153).

tive in the urban setting in which most people are destined to live out their lives? Merton's answer would be: only with great, if not insurmountable, difficulty. In a celebrated passage, which impresses more by its earnestness than its practicability, Merton suggests how one may try to find solitude in the city.

Do everything you can to avoid the amusement and the noise and the business of men. Keep as far away as you can from the places where they gather to cheat and insult one another, to exploit one another, to laugh at one another, or to mock one another with their false gestures of friendship. Do not read their newspapers, if you can help it. Be glad if you can keep beyond the reach of their radios. Do not bother with their unearthly songs or their intolerable concerns for the way their bodies look and feel.

Do not smoke their cigarettes or drink the things they drink or share their preoccupation with different kinds of food. Do not complicate your life by looking at the pictures in their magazines.

Keep your eyes clean and your ears quiet and your mind serene. Breathe God's air. Work, if you can, under His sky.

But if you have to live in a city and work among machines and ride in the subways and eat in a place where the radio makes you deaf with spurious news and where the food destroys your life and the sentiments of those around you poison your heart with boredom, do not be upset, but accept it as the love of God and as a seed of solitude planted in your soul, and be glad of this suffering; for it will keep you alive to the next opportunity to escape from them and be alone in the healing silence of recollection and in the untroubled presence of God.*

---

*The exuberant *contemptus mundi* of this passage is toned down slightly in the December 1949 revision of *Seeds of Contemplation* and extensively so in *New Seeds of Contemplation* (1962). The writer is persuaded, however, that Merton never retreated from its basic thrust.

Actualizing my capacities for contemplation requires an existential freedom which liberates me from the illusion of my false self that would keep me living in a world of unreality. It requires a moral freedom that detaches me from the selfish desires, cares, and ambitions—even spiritual ones—that interfere with my search for God.

There is yet another type of freedom needed for the contemplative experience, and that is what Merton calls intellectual freedom, or the freedom from concepts and images of created things. For the goal of contemplation is to meet at my center God as He is in Himself. And yet "we cannot know Him as He really is unless we pass beyond everything that can be imagined and enter into an obscurity without images and without the likeness of any created thing."

Really to meet God means that we have to pass beyond the kataphatic way that seeks to find Him mirrored in the perfections of His creatures. "No matter what you predicate of Him, you have to add that He is not what we conceive by that term." The apophatic way of meeting God in the darkness is the shorter and simpler way. For the living God is not a philosopher's abstraction. "He lies beyond the reach of anything our eyes can see or our minds can understand." Neither is He the God the theologians speak of in the dogmas of faith. For the Truth of God as He is in Himself is apprehended "not in distinct and clear-cut definitions but in the limpid obscurity of a single intuition that unites all dogmas in one simple Light, shining into the soul directly from God's eternity, without the medium of created concept, without the intervention of symbols or of language or the likenesses of material things."

The only One who can truly know God is God Himself. If we are to know Him as He is in Himself, we must in some way be transformed into Him. We must become somehow what He is. This is to say that the highest freedom possible to us is to know God as He is in Himself by loving identification with Him in obscurity. The seeds "planted in my liberty" turn out to be not only the seeds of my identity but the seeds of my identification with God.

Merton's obvious preference for the "shorter and simpler way" of apophaticism is evidenced by the more than fifty references to "darkness" (or its equivalents: "night," "cloud," "obscurity") that appear in *Seeds of Contemplation*.

For Merton, all the exercises of the spiritual life (reading, meditation, etc.) are intended to lead us into the darkness. Thus, he says of meditation: If it "only produces images and ideas and affections that you can understand and feel and appreciate, it is not yet doing its full quota of work." Meditation achieves its purpose when it brings you to a point of bafflement and darkness, wherein you can no longer think of God or imagine Him and "are consequently forced to reach out to Him by blind faith, and hope and love." When you reach this point you must not be discouraged by the seeming futility of meditation; instead, you should relax "in a simple contemplative gaze that keeps your attention peacefully aware of Him hidden somewhere in this deep cloud," into which you have entered.

Entering this cloud of darkness awakens our spirit to a new level of experience. This awakening is so unique an experience that by comparison the sharpest natural experience is like sleep. It is an awakening to the full possession of God, whom we yet possess in the darkness. For "our minds are most truly liberated from the weak created lights that are darkness in comparison to Him and we are filled with His infinite Light which is pure darkness to us."

In the darkness the last vestiges of selfishness are taken away. "The deep and secret selfishness that is too close for us to identify is stripped away from our souls" and in the darkness we are made free.

The darkness becomes an atmosphere of breathless clarity in which we find peace, and the deep night becomes the brightness of the noonday sun, in which we find the One whom alone our heart desires. And we find ourselves on the threshold of a totally new experience, where we are no longer the subjects of an experience but are the experience itself. The duality between God and ourselves disappears.

Merton attempts to clarify what this means:

> What happens is that the separate entity that was *you* suddenly disappears and nothing is left but a pure freedom indistinguishable from infinite Freedom. Love identified with Love. Not two loves, one waiting for the other, striving for the other, seeking for the other, but Love Loving in Freedom.

Contemplation finally becomes what it is really meant to be:

> It is no longer something poured out of God into a created subject, so much as God living in God and identifying a created life with His own Life so that there is nothing left of any significance but God living in God.

III

The Ascent to Truth

In his first writing on contemplation, the booklet *What Is Contemplation,* Merton makes use of the writings of St. Thomas Aquinas and St. John of the Cross to explain what contemplation is and how to deal with the gift of contemplation when one receives it. This early work was too brief to allow for any detailed understanding of the teachings of the Angelic Doctor or of the saint of Carmel. Merton's obvious interest in what these two saints had to say about contemplation blossomed into a book called *The Ascent to Truth. The Ascent to Truth* attempts to combine the scholasticism of St. Thomas with the mystical doctrine of St. John of the Cross, whom Merton calls the "safest" of mystical theologians.

Merton began work on this book probably sometime in December of 1948. Its original title was *The Cloud and the Fire.* There is evidence, in *The Sign of Jonas,* that he encountered more than ordinary difficulty in writing it. Thus, he records on February 9, 1949:

My work has been tied up in knots for two months—more. I have been trying to write *The Cloud and the Fire,* which is a book about contemplation and the theology of contemplation at that. The theology of contemplation does not mix with fan mail. Also it is difficult . . . I have a huge mass of half-digested notes, all mixed up, and I can't find my way around in them. My ideas are not fixed and clear . . .

Six days later, on February 15, he writes:

I had been thinking of tearing up *The Cloud and the Fire* for a long time. I haven't done that exactly, but I have simply stuffed it into an envelope, plans and all, and reconsidered what it was I was supposed to start.

About *The Cloud and the Fire*—I have in mind something that needs to be done some day: the dogmatic essentials of mystical theology based on tradition and delivered in the context and atmosphere of Scripture and the liturgy.

On February 20, 1949, he writes, in a more optimistic frame of mind: "With Our Lady's help the book, now changed and called *The School of the Spirit,* goes quite smoothly." This mood did not last for long. On April 29, 1949, he speaks once again of his frustration:

I wonder how many plans I have made for this book, *The School of the Spirit?* Perhaps six—including the ones I made for it when it was called *The Cloud and the Fire.* * So I sit at the typewriter, with my fingers all wound up in a cat's cradle of strings, overwhelmed with the sense of my own stupidity and surrounded by not one but a multitude of literary dilemmas.

Sifting through some eight hundred pages of notes in different notebooks, he could not quite decide how to put them together.

---

*"The Cloud and the Fire" is the title of the first of the three sections of *The Ascent to Truth.*

This business of "getting my notes together" is something that can go on absolutely interminably, because there exists an almost unlimited number of combinations in which you can arrange the statements you have jotted down so carefully on some eight hundred pages of various notebooks.

All that undigested material is utterly terrifying, and fascinating at the same time.

Merton failed to complete *The School of the Spirit* in 1949. On January 7, 1950, he wrote to Sister Therese Lentfoehr: "I do not mean to drop *The School of the Spirit* entirely. Only to take it up again from a more thorough Scriptural and Patristic viewpoint later on." A year later, on January 8, 1951, he confided to Sister Therese that the book he had been writing "finally split into two that can be easier finished than one. This will content the publisher and save the author a few headaches." The first part of the original book, which retained the title *The School of the Spirit,* was never completed, at least not to Merton's satisfaction.* The second part, which dealt with the doctrine of St. John of the Cross, became *The Ascent to Truth.*

The *Ascent to Truth* exhibits some of the battle scars Merton experienced in writing it. It does not read with the smoothness of *Seeds of Contemplation;* at times it is overly speculative and repetitious. There are lingering elements of the "Catholic" narrowness that at times beclouds *The Seven Storey Mountain* and *The Secular Journal;* e.g., in his chapter on "The Problem of Unbelief." One wonders, too, whether Merton in his later years would have made the sweeping statement: "Theology is not made by mystics; mystics are formed by theology." Certainly it is true that

---

*In the Trust Agreement, Merton stated that *The School of the Spirit* was not to be published as a book. What actually remains of *The School of the Spirit* is something of a mystery. The writer has seen two typescripts of it that are totally different from each other.

mysticism cannot flourish in a theological vacuum, but does not the mystic have important data from his own experience to offer the theologian for his reflection? Did not St. Thomas draw on the insights of mystics of the Patristic Age? Is it true to say that the mysticism of St. John of the Cross was formed by the theology of St. Thomas, or would it be more correct to say that his mystical life was formed by God and that the saint used the terminology of St. Thomas to articulate his experience?

In the comparative graph he made in 1967 evaluating a number of his books, Merton described *The Ascent to Truth* as only "Fair." It is difficult to fault his own evaluation.

To suggest shortcomings in the book is not to deny that it has value. His clarification of the ways of darkness and light in contemplation, the soundness of the ascetical discipline he presents, his description of the value and limitations of conceptual knowledge of God, his insistence on the crucial role played by our intelligence in the various stages that lead to contemplative union, his careful nuancing of the relationship between intelligence and love in the experience of God, the insights into the meaning of the Prayer of Quiet, Transforming Union and the Beatific Vision he offers—all these elements of the book are of perennial concern to anyone interested in the contemplative vision of reality.

Yet the fact remains that this book has not the appeal of his earlier work, *Seeds of Contemplation;* nor did it fare so well with the critics or the general public.* The limpid simplicity of *Seeds* is missing from *The Ascent to Truth.* Perhaps one explanation of the difference between these two works is the different perspective from which each was written. Merton in all he wrote was very much of a traditionalist; that

---

*See, e.g., the review of *The Ascent to Truth* in *Blackfriars* 33:144–46 (March 1952).

is to say, he always wrote with the utmost respect for the Christian tradition (and, in his later years, for other religious traditions). Sometimes he wrote out of the background of his own tradition, filtering that tradition through his own mind (as he did in *Seeds of Contemplation*); at other times he wrote *about* that tradition (e.g., in *The Ascent to Truth*). He was more successful in doing the first than the second. In writing *about* the tradition, he seems at times to be submerged in it and to become abstract and unduly speculative; in writing *out of the background* of the tradition, he is more truly himself, more concrete, more existential, more accessible. Despite the breadth of his learning, Merton is not at his best in writing scholarly works. Indeed, one of the problems of *The Ascent to Truth* is that it is difficult to be sure what readers he had in mind. The book is hardly scholarly enough for the professional theologian and almost too scholarly, in some sections at least, for the general reader.

In *The Ascent to Truth,* Merton sets for himself three main goals: (1) to define the nature of the contemplative experience; (2) to show the necessary ascetical discipline leading to that experience; and (3) to give a brief sketch of mature contemplation. In working toward these goals, Merton draws on the principal writings of St. John of the Cross *(The Ascent of Mount Carmel, The Dark Night of the Soul, The Spiritual Canticle,* and *The Living Flame).* He links the teaching of the Carmelite saint with the teachings of St. Thomas Aquinas, particularly with the five opening questions of the *Prima Secundae* of the *Summa Theologica,* wherein St. Thomas sketches his outline of the meaning of happiness and locates our last end in the highest contemplation of God. This Thomistic teaching, Merton says, "not only influenced St. John of the Cross, but actually provided him with the basic structure of his whole doctrine." He adds:

"The mere fact that St. John of the Cross was able to see the tremendous implications, for the contemplative life on earth, contained in a few simple, fundamental ideas of the Angelic Doctor about man's last end, is itself evidence of St. John's theological genius."

John's ascetical teaching, that complete detachment from creatures is necessary before one can arrive at union with God, builds on the doctrine of St. Thomas that our last end cannot be found in anything created. His mystical teaching, that the goal of the spiritual quest consists in contemplative union with God beyond concepts and images in the darkness of faith in this life and in the perfection of vision in the life to come, is but a reprise of St. Thomas's theme that our happiness consists in nothing less than the vision of the very essence of God.

The three goals Merton set for himself are not always developed in successive order, though they correspond roughly to the three divisions of the book: they are, rather, goals that pervade his text and at times overlap with one another. Nor is the link he attempts to forge between the theology of St. Thomas and the mysticism of St. John of the Cross presented in any systematic way. He relates the one to the other as it suits the purpose of the particular chapter he is writing. Though there is a development in the book, a number of the chapters appear to be almost separate essays that could be read on their own.*

This lack of any tidy developmental sequence in the book makes it difficult to try to summarize its contents in a few pages. In an attempt to bring a measure of unity into the

---

*Merton's statement in *The Sign of Jonas* (quoted earlier) about the unlimited number of combinations possible for the statements he had jotted down in some eight hundred pages of notes suggests that the final arrangement of that material may well have been somewhat arbitrary.

discussion of a lengthy and somewhat complicated book, I have chosen to confine this summary to two topics which represent main thrusts in the book: (1) the *moral asceticism* of St. John of the Cross, by which I mean his teaching on the detachment that is so essential to the contemplative journey; and (2) his *intellectual asceticism,* by which I mean his insistence on the proper discipline of the intellect at the beginning of the journey toward God, during the course of that journey, and even when its summit has been reached. This second topic is a special emphasis for Merton, because he was firmly convinced that "there is no such thing as a sanctity that is not intelligent."

The moral asceticism of St. John of the Cross is an uncompromising call for complete detachment from creatures in order to arrive at union with God. It is an asceticism that is based on the teaching of St. Thomas Aquinas that our happiness cannot be found in creatures. In question two of the *Prima Secundae* of his *Summa Theologica,* St. Thomas examines one by one the created goods that one might look to for happiness—material possessions, honor, fame, power, pleasure, bodily health, the natural perfection of the soul—and he finds them all wanting. No created reality can constitute human happiness. To be happy, one must be taken out of himself, not simply to a higher order of creation, but to the uncreated reality of God Himself. God alone is our happiness.

But a person can seek his happiness in God only if he is not seeking it in creatures. This is to say, he must be detached from creatures. In what does this detachment consist? Some might be tempted to say that it means total withdrawal from creatures insofar as this is possible. This is not the answer of St. John of the Cross. He is no gnostic: he denies neither the goodness of creatures nor the need to use them. He probes deeper to the very roots of the problem posed by creatures. The problem is not in creatures but in ourselves. It is not creatures but the *desire* for them that impedes our quest for God. John affirms without reservation "that the desire of creatures as ends in themselves cannot coexist with the desire of God as our true end." The ascetical task is to rid ourselves, not of creatures, but of the desire to pursue them for their own sake apart from God.

The words that follow are St. John's call to detachment. They are lines which, Merton says, "have proved to be a terror and a scandal to many Christians":

> In order to have pleasure in everything
> Desire to have pleasure in nothing.
>
> In order to arrive at possessing everything
> Desire to possess nothing.
>
> In order to arrive at being everything
> Desire to be nothing.
>
> In order to arrive at knowing everything
> Desire to know nothing.

Merton's comments on these lines of St. John of the Cross are splendid:

> Todo y Nada. All and nothing. The two words contain the theology of St. John of the Cross. Todo—all—is God, Who contains in Himself eminently the perfections of all things. For Him we are made. In Him we possess all things. But in order to possess Him Who is all, we must renounce the possession of anything that is less than God. But everything that can be seen, known, enjoyed, possessed in a finite manner, is less than God. Every desire for knowledge, possession, being that falls short of God must be blacked out. *Nada!*

John is not wasting words, Merton warns us. We have to read him with close attention, as with merciless objectivity he identifies the enemy. It is not pleasure or possession or knowledge. It is DESIRE. The secret of ascetical liberation is "the darkening of desire." As Merton points out, John does not say: "In order to arrive at the knowledge of everything, *know* nothing," but *"desire to know* nothing." It is not pleasure, knowledge, possession, or being as such that must be "darkened" and "mortified," but only the passion of desire for these things.

It is only by the "blacking out" of desire that we can begin to fulfill the greatest of the commandments: to love God with our whole heart, our whole soul and our whole strength. And for St. John this commandment sums up the entire ascetical and mystical life.

Yet the passion of desire is strong and imperious in the human psyche. The ultimate perversion of that passion is reached when, instead of seeking creatures for the sake of creatures, one seeks desire for the sake of desire. A person may pursue created goods as goals that he hopes will bring him happiness. When one does not satisfy, he tries another, and another. Finally, unable to locate happiness in anything he pursues, he may try to seek it in the very pursuit itself. Even when we see the futility of what we desire, we may continue to desire for the sake of desiring. The chase for pleasure then becomes the very pleasure that we seek. We become like persons who run all day to catch a hare they would probably not accept as a gift. Desire for the sake of desire becomes a diversion, whereby we fling ourselves into exterior activities for their own sake—activities that benumb our spirits and distract us from the emptiness of our lives.

Desire—whether it be the desire for a particular creature or desire turned back on itself—locks us in a prison of falsity and illusion from which we can be delivered only by discernment in the intellect and detachment in the will.

Discernment in the intellect and detachment in the will

—both are necessary equipment for the ascetical journey. We cannot be freed from the desire for creatures until we know what creatures are and why it is futile to make them the object of desire. This is the task of discernment: it breaks through the spider's web of illusion that desire spins around creatures, and reveals creatures in their true light. Discernment does not tell us that creatures are not good but only that they are not good enough to satisfy the longings of the human heart. Discernment gives eyes to detachment. Guided by the light of discernment, detachment frees us from all desires not centered on God. It delivers us from absorption in what is accidental and transitory. It refuses to let us be submerged by what is in ultimate terms trivial and insignificant.

Discernment, by exposing creatures for what they are, and detachment, by disarming vain desires that would lead us astray, make us capable of a knowledge that is serene and a joy that is incorruptible. And we experience this serene knowledge and incorruptible joy not only in God but also in creatures. For once our knowledge and love find their fulfillment in God, we become free to find and enjoy in Him the whole of His creation.

> Desiring to have pleasure in nothing
> we have pleasure in everything.

> Desiring to possess nothing
> we arrive at possessing everything.

> Desiring to know nothing
> we arrive at knowing everything.

Far from teaching us to hate this world, John of the Cross tells us the way to love it and understand it. Paradoxically, we are able to be happy with creatures only when we no longer look to them as the source of our happiness.

The end of all ascetical discipline is freedom: the mind's freedom from illusion (achieved through discernment), and the will's freedom from desire (achieved through detachment). When we possess this freedom, we can know creatures and love them, without any fear that they will lead us away from God; for we have found them in Him.

Contemplation is an experience of God that exceeds our natural capabilities. It is union with God beyond images and concepts, realized in this life in Pure Faith and in heaven in the beatific vision.

Though this union with God which is the highest possible experience of Him is beyond our natural powers, it is nonetheless true that the human intellect plays an important role—at the beginning and along the way—in our progressive ascent toward union with God. So does the human will. As has already been pointed out, one of Merton's principal concerns in *The Ascent to Truth* is to clarify the role of intelligence in the contemplative journey and its relation to love.

The intellect has a role to play at the very beginning of the spiritual journey. Before we can go beyond images and concepts, we must have images and concepts to go beyond. By the natural power of human reason, we can arrive at a true, albeit limited, knowledge of God. We can know God in the concepts that come to us from created things. For all created things reflect the reality of God. They are footprints showing that God has passed by. The problem, of course, is that created things are but dim, imperfect, partial reflections of who God is. They tell us only that He has been there, not where He has gone. Concepts derived from created things are, therefore, never adequate to grasp the reality of God. They are limited, His reality is unlimited.

Indeed, our concepts are limited even when we use them to signify created things. Concepts, though they give us an intellectual grasp of reality, are incapable of conveying the total concreteness of the reality they describe. Of necessity, they have limits and boundaries. If they did not have limits, we would not understand them. We define a tree differently from the way we define a horse. To define or conceptualize something is to place limits on it. The root of the English word "define" is the Latin word "finis," which means limit or limitation. To "de-fine"—that is, to place limits on something—is to say that it is "this," not something else. What we cannot define—that is, put limits on—we cannot know. Thus, to take an example, we can know wisdom and justice insofar as they are different things. If we were to say that wisdom and justice are the same thing, one concept (or definition) would cancel out the other and neither would have meaning for us.

The limited character of all created concepts would seem to pose an insoluble problem when we try to rise from these concepts to a knowledge of God. The Reality of God is one and undivided; it is unlimited. How can our diverse and limited concepts grasp in any way the undivided and unlimited Reality of God?

St. Thomas's way out of this dilemma is his teaching on the analogy of being—an approach to God that involves not only affirmation but also denial. Analogy means that the concepts we have of created things are verified in God, but always in a way different from the way they are true of creatures. As Merton writes:

> It is impossible for us to understand the notions of justice and mercy unless they are somehow divided from one another and opposed. In God justice is mercy, mercy is justice and both are wisdom and power and being, for all His attributes merge in one infinite Reality that elevates them beyond definition and comprehension.

Every concept, therefore, that reason proposes to us about God tells us two things: (1) insofar as it is actually true of Him, it tells us *what He is:* He is wise, just, merciful; (2) insofar as it is not true of Him in any anthropomorphic or limited sense, it tells us *what He is not.*

Thus, there are two ways of approaching God through concepts: the way of affirmation and the way of denial; and we need both. In Merton's words:

> We must affirm and deny at the same time. One cannot go without the other. If we go on affirming without denying, we end up by affirming that we have delimited the Being of God in our concepts. If we go on denying without affirming, we end up by denying that our concepts can tell the truth about Him in any way whatever.

In a helpful image, Merton compares the ways of affirmation and denial to the takeoff and the flight of a plane. We make a statement about God: we affirm that He exists. This is the plane taking off. The plane rolls along the ground: we apply existence to God in the way it applies to us. But only for the moment. For, having affirmed, we now have to deny. The plane takes off into the air. It can do so only by "renouncing" its contact with the ground. So we cannot reach God in our concepts unless we renounce their limits and definitions. We take off from the "ground" of our affirmation and ascend into the "sky" of our denials. We know God—but imperfectly—in our affirmations. We know Him—but darkly—in our denials. Knowing God in our denials is to know Him by "unknowing."

While reason through its affirmations and denials can speak to us of God as His reality is imagined in creatures, it cannot by itself make contact with God as He is in Himself. It can, however, tell us that such contact is possible. When it has made known all that creatures can say about

God, and therefore can go no further by its own light, reason can tell that, over and above "the footprints He has left behind Him as He went on His way," there is another light that can tell us where He has gone and where He is. This is the light of faith. Reason, admitting its own limitations, can yet show us "that the only one who can tell us anything about God (as He is in Himself) is God Himself." It can make known to us that God is able to communicate Himself to us so that what we cannot know about Him by ourselves we can know through His self-communication.

Faith is our response to this self-communication of God. It enables our intelligence "to make a firm and complete assent to divinely revealed truths, not on account of the clear intrinsic evidence of the statements about God, but on the authority of God revealing." By faith we adhere to what we do not actually see; hence, the act of faith is not purely intellectual. It is elicited under the impulsion of the will. Because we believe what we do not see, faith is dark; because we believe under the impulsion of the will, faith is loving. That is why St. John of the Cross speaks of "this dark and loving knowledge which is faith."

The object of faith is not simply propositions about God, but God Himself. "Faith terminates in God in the sense that every article of revealed truth ends in God or refers to God." What faith attains to, therefore, is not just *God revealed* in the statements of faith, but *God revealing,* namely, God as He is in Himself.

Insofar as the object of faith is *God revealed to us,* faith is able to be expressed in propositions that tell us things about God that are beyond reason's light. Reason, while not able to arrive at these propositions by itself, can nevertheless reflect on them once they have been revealed. This it does in speculative theology and especially in meditation. Moved by love, we become absorbed in new concepts about

God that faith reveals. We thrill at a whole new level of understanding that opens up before us. New insights lead to new affective experiences of God and we go out to God in a deeper and more ardent love. Every new insight into God's reality becomes another reason for loving Him.

Yet we cannot rest content simply with propositions about God. Faith attains not only to God revealed (in the propositions of faith) but to God revealing (that is, known in Himself, but in the darkness). Propositions are still concepts about God: they cannot reach Him as He is in Himself. They cannot unite us with God. Hence, while it is good to seek God in concepts, it is futile to expect that any conceptual knowledge, even that of faith, can lead us to union with God as He is in Himself.

That is why a person has to know when the time has come to go beyond concepts into the dark but truer knowledge of God that lies beyond them. This is the moment when reason has to say no to reasoning. It is the moment when concepts have to become the diving board from which, at His bidding, we spring into the abyss of God. The call to contemplation is an invitation to turn our awareness of God from what is revealed about Him to Him who offers the revelation. This is the call to move from knowing God with clear concepts to knowing Him in the darkness of "unknowing." We must allow the small matches which are our concepts ("intelligence," "love," "power") to be blown out by the tremendous reality of God bearing down upon us like a dark storm. We must plunge with abandon into the Darkness of Pure Faith, where the soul knows God, "not because it beholds Him face to face, but because it is touched by Him in darkness."

> Faith takes man beyond the limits of his own finite intelligence. It is therefore "dark" to him, because he has no

longer any faculty with which to see the infinite Truth of God.

The way of Pure Faith is also the way of Love. In the darkness in which we do not see God, we are united to Him in the act of love. And this love of God in contemplative prayer makes a positive contribution to our knowledge of Him. For "it gives the soul concrete possession of everything that is contained in the truths of faith."

> Love gives an experience, a taste of what we have not seen and are not yet able to see. Faith gives us a full title to this treasure which is ours to possess in darkness. Love enters the darkness and lays hands upon what is its own!

In the darkness of Pure Faith, love gives us a positive experience of the transcendent quality of God's perfections which the propositions of faith can express only in a negative way. Thus, faith can tell us that God is good, but it must also add that God's goodness infinitely transcends all our ideas of goodness. Love can give us "a direct, positive experience of that abundant goodness which concepts could only declare to be beyond their knowledge." That is why love is able to astound the intellect

> with vivid reports of a transcendent Actuality which minds can only know, on earth, by a confession of ignorance. And so, when the mind admits that God is too great for our knowledge, love replies: "I know Him."

These words of Merton are a beautiful and moving expression of love's experience plunged into the midnight of Dark Faith, but they are a poetic description and we must not overliteralize them. Though love's experience is real (it really touches God and is touched by Him), yet, strictly speaking, it is not knowledge. It is knowing by "unknowing." It is possession, but possession of what is not known. That is why it can never entirely satisfy the yearnings of the human soul.

> Just as conceptual knowledge creates anguish in the contemplative by reminding him how little he knows of God, so the possession of God by love, on earth, fills him with still greater agony, because it tells him that he can only rest in vision.

Possessing God in the darkness by love is a far deeper experience than knowing Him in the limited concepts of the intellect; yet possessing Him in darkness only makes us yearn more fully to see Him face to face. "Love does not heal our ignorance; mystical love is a sickness which vision alone can cure." Even at the highest level of the mystical life, the experience of Transforming Union, "love cries out with a more and more ardent hunger and sweetly demands the satiation of perfect vision."

This perfect vision which the soul, transformed in God, awaits at the threshold of heaven is

> a clear intuition which in one glance takes in and, in a certain measure, comprehends everything that is obscurely revealed, in fragmentary fashion, by all the articles of faith, by all the truths revealed by God and even by the truths about God and His creation which reason can grasp.

This is the summit of the mystical journey. It is seeing God, not through a glass darkly, but face to face, and knowing Him as He knows Himself.

As was made clear earlier, a point is reached in the contemplative ascent to God when the would-be contemplative realizes that he must abandon concepts of God in order to plunge into the darkness of Pure Faith. Two questions remain to be discussed: (1) what are the signs that identify the moment in the spiritual journey when one should stop seeking God by concepts; and (2) once we have entered into the contemplative experience in Pure Faith and Love, does reason quietly remove itself from the scene, or does it still have its role to play?

St. John of the Cross suggests three signs which can help the soul to decide that it is ready to drop discursive meditation and the effort to reach God by concepts. The first sign is the inability any longer to engage in fruitful meditation. Meditation which once brought joy to the soul becomes hard and wearisome. The second sign is a lack of interest in particular ways of representing God. Particular representations of God in the mind or the imagination, in a statue or a picture, no longer inspire devotion in the soul. This is a critical moment in a person's spiritual life. It means "the soul has come face to face with the distinction between God in Himself and God as He is contained in our concepts of Him," and the first is immeasurably more attractive than the second. There is a growing distaste for representations of God "which are powerless to do justice to His infinite reality." The third sign is a positive attraction for solitary contemplative prayer. In the words of St. John:

> The third and surest sign is that the soul takes pleasure in being alone and waits with loving attentiveness upon God, without any particular meditation, in inner peace and quietness and rest.

What St. John is describing is not a state of passivity. The soul is still engaged in an activity of the mind which is quite definite and precise; namely, attentiveness to God. "The difference" Merton suggests, "is not between activity and inactivity, but between two kinds of activity—between reasoning and intuition. The soul gazes with the desire of love into the darkness where God is hidden and gradually loses sight of every other object."

What is the role of reason when the soul crosses the divide between discursive meditation and the contemplative striving for God beyond concepts?* Its first task is to determine whether or not the moment has arrived to take this step. St. John of the Cross has laid down the guidelines; but guidelines must be applied. It is reason that makes the application. Reason gives the "go-ahead" to move to a higher level of the ascent to God.†

Reason must continue to operate in the Night of Faith. It must keep the contemplative traveling along the straight road of faith that leads to divine union. There is a type of mysticism that can lead people astray—a mysticism that thrives on unusual spiritual experiences; revelations or locutions or visions. St. John of the Cross does not deny that God can communicate with the soul of the mystic in these ways; but he does insist that such experiences should neither be sought after nor desired, since they cannot help us to know God as He really is. It is here that reason plays a decisive role. It must sift critically all spiritual experiences and reject those that fall outside the realms of Pure Faith. "Reason, acting in the service of faith, must question and evaluate and pass judgment on all our most intimate and spiritual aspirations."

The great paradox of St. John of the Cross is that his asceticism of "night" cannot possibly be practiced without

---

*It should be clear that this "divide" is not crossed once and for all. There may be times when one who has tasted the joy of the contemplative life may experience the need for meditation.
†Obviously, reason does not do this apart from or independently of the inspirations of God's grace.

the *light of reason.* It is by the light of reason that we keep on traveling through the night of faith.

Merton compares the soul's journey along the way of Pure Faith to the journey of a car along a dark road at night. The driver can keep to the road only by using his head-lights.

> The way of faith is necessarily obscure . . . We drive by night. Nevertheless, our reason penetrates the darkness enough to show us a little of the road ahead. It is by the light of reason that we interpret the signposts and make out the landmarks along our way.

Reason's task, therefore, in the ascent toward union with God, is to remove anything that would hinder the soul from receiving the inspiration of God. St. Gregory Nazianzen calls the soul of the contemplative "an instrument played by the Holy Spirit." From this instrument the Holy Spirit can bring forth harmonies and melodies we could never have dreamed of hearing. Reason's work is not to play the instrument but to tune the strings.

> The Master Himself does not waste time tuning the instruments. He shows His servant, reason, how to do it and leaves him to do the work. If He then comes and finds the piano still out of tune, He does not bother to play anything on it.

Reason must judge the right measure of self-denial that will keep the soul responsive to the "keys when they are struck by God." By the active work of discrimination, which elimi-nates the movements of disordered passion and ill-regulated instincts, reason disposes the soul for passive union with God.

We have seen already how reason exercises its power of discrimination in the Night of Sense by enabling us to see what creatures are and what they are not. But its highest powers of discrimination are reserved for the Night of the Spirit, in which it helps us to discern what is and what is not of God. This is reason's highest function and its greatest glory.

Enough has been said to show the important place that St. John of the Cross assigns to reason in the life of contemplation. "Enter," he says, "into account with thy reason to do that which it counsels thee on the road to God, and it will be of greater worth to thee with respect to God than all the works thou doest without this counsel." Reason serving under the standard of faith is an indispensable servant in our struggle for perfection. By reason alone, we can never hope to achieve union with God; but neither can we hope to achieve it without reason. To repeat Merton's words, quoted earlier: "There is no such thing as a sanctity that is not intelligent."

IV

The Inner Experience:
An Overview

During the summer of 1959, Merton produced a full-length book devoted to the topic of contemplation. Previously, as has been pointed out, he had written a brief systematic study of contemplation that appeared in 1948 as a small booklet entitled *What Is Contemplation.* The following year he had written a series of personal notes and reflections called *Seeds of Contemplation.* Two years later (1951) appeared *The Ascent to Truth,* a study of the mystical theology of St. John of the Cross. Because of his keen interest in the contemplative experience, it was inevitable that sooner or later he would write a full-length, systematic study of the meaning of contemplation. This he did in the summer of 1959 in a book called *The Inner Experience.* *

The Inner Experience was initially intended to be a revision of *What Is Contemplation.* On July 4, 1959, Merton wrote to Sister Therese Lentfoehr: "At the moment, guess what, I

---

*The title that Merton originally chose for the work was *The Dark Path.*

am rewriting *What Is Contemplation.* It will be a patchy job. But I have been wanting to do it. I may revise other early material too."*Merton confided to Sister Therese his reason for wanting to revise some of his earlier writing: "It is all very unsatisfactory to me. In fact a lot of it disgusts me. I was much too superficial and too cerebral at the time. I seem to have ignored the wholeness and integrity of life, and concentrated on a kind of angelism in contemplation. That was when I was a rip-roaring Trappist, I guess. Now that I am a little less perfect I seem to have a saner perspective. And that too seems to be not according to the manuals, doesn't it?"

Merton apparently spent a great deal of time during the summer of 1959 working on this revision of *What Is Contemplation.* On September 29, 1959, he was able to report to Sister Therese: "I finished a book this summer called *The Inner Experience,* which started out to be a simple revision of *What Is Contemplation,* but turned into something new, and just about full-length." Although he stated that he had finished the book, he was apparently not satisfied with it. For he goes on to say: "It has to be revised and has been sitting here on the desk waiting for revision for some time, but I refuse to work around the house as they are blasting around on all sides with jackhammers and other machines and it is impossible to think. The novices have been making a good share of this noise, trying to put a couple of new showers in our crowded cellar." Presumably the new showers were installed and the jackhammers and machines even-

---

*This would suggest that *The Inner Experience,* besides including the booklet *What Is Contemplation,* contains other material written before 1959. The writer is persuaded that some such earlier material has been incorporated into *The Inner Experience,* but is unable to identify it or its source.

tually stopped their blasting, but Merton never got around to revising the manuscript of *The Inner Experience.*

The manuscript that Merton wrote survives in four typescripts that are housed at the Thomas Merton Studies Center at Bellarmine College in Louisville, Kentucky. The first draft is made up almost entirely of new material into which Merton apparently intended to insert the contents of *What Is Contemplation.* The second draft contains some material from the earlier work. Draft 3 has in it about ninety percent of the text of *What Is Contemplation.* Draft 4 is identical with the third draft except that pages 77 and 78 are numbered in the fourth draft as pages 77a and 77b. This means that the pagination of draft 4 from this point is one page off from the pagination of draft 3. Thus, draft 3 runs to 151 pages; draft 4, only to 150. Draft 4 also differs from the third draft in that it has a number of handwritten notations added to the text.*

Two diagrams follow. The first (A) indicates the relationship of the four drafts to one another in terms of their content. The second diagram (B) shows the common material between *The Inner Experience* (draft 4) and *What Is Contemplation.*

This chapter is intended to present a brief overview of the contents of *The Inner Experience.* The text used will be the fourth draft. As diagram A indicates, there is some confusion about the division of *The Inner Experience* into

---

*The writer is of the opinion that the third draft is actually the fourth, since in it the pagination is corrected (pages 77a and 77b of the "fourth" draft becoming pages 77 and 78). If this opinion is correct, Merton's handwritten notations were made on what in fact was the third draft. This is quite possible, because drafts 3 and 4 are identical in content; hence, it would have made little difference which draft he chose to annotate. Note: reference in this work to the different drafts will follow the accepted designations.

chapters. There are two Chapters IV. Merton then skips to Chapter VII. Following Chapter VII are two unnumbered chapters which one would expect to be Chapters VIII and IX; yet they are followed by a chapter numbered IX. Chapter X to XV follow in order.

For the purpose of study, *The Inner Experience* may conveniently be divided into three almost equal sections, in terms of Merton's original intent to revise *What Is Contemplation:* (A) The first section (pp. 1–54, including Chapters I to IV), in which Merton is dealing mostly with new material.*(B) The middle section (pp. 55–103, including the second Chapter IV, Chapter VII, two unnumbered chapters, Chapters IX and X), in which Merton attempts, not always successfully, to combine the contents of *What Is Contemplation* with new material.†(C) The last section (pp. 104–150, including Chapters XI to XV), in which once again he is dealing with new material.

THE FIRST SECTION OF THE INNER EXPERIENCE

In a world threatened by moral and emotional chaos, there are those who would hold out to us the promise of a bright future. Popular psychologists, religious teachers, and people of pathetic optimism fret over our distressing tendency to see the dark side of modern life and seek to inspire and uplift us. They point to the remarkable progress we have made in raising our standard of living and providing for ourselves leisure time unheard of in previous generations.

*Chapter IV deals with some material from *What Is Contemplation.* See diagram B.
†The ambiguities of this section may well be the reason for Merton's directive in the indenture to his will that *The Inner Experience* not be published as a book.

Diagram A: THE INNER EXPERIENCE

Diagram A: THE INNER EXPERIENCE

Diagram B

THE INNER EXPERIENCE (4th draft-150 pages)	Common Material	WHAT IS CONTEMPLATION (1978 Templegate ed.- 78 small pages)
I. A Preliminary Warning p. 1–5		What is Contemplation p. 7–12
II. The Awakening of the Inner Self 6–17		
III. Society and the Inner Self 17–33		
IV. Christian Contemplation 34–54		
1. Contemplation and Theology 36–41		
2. Contemplation and the Gospels 41–47	45–46 14–18	The Promises of Christ 14–20
	46–47 21–24	St. Thomas Aquinas 21–26
Sacred and Secular 48–54	53–54 24	
IV. Kinds of Contemplation 55–69		Kinds of Contemplation 27–35
		Active Contemplation 27–29
Liturgy 59–62	62 30–33	Liturgy 29–33
Union with God in Activity 62–65	62–63 33–35	Union with God in Activity 33–35
Acquired and Infused Contemplation 65–66		
Natural Contemplation and Mystical Theology 66–69		
VII. Infused Contemplation 70–89	72–75 36–42	Infused Contemplation 35–44
		St. Bernard of Clairvaux 37–38
		"A Ray of Darkness 38–44
Five Texts on Contemplative Prayer 78–84		The Test 45–54
The Paradox of the Illuminative Way 85–89	84–85 47–53	Peace, Recollection Desire 46–54

With a dash of psychological self-help and a decent minimum of religious conformity, they would help us adjust ourselves to the emptiness of life so characteristic of our age.

In such a situation, Merton asks: Does one dare suggest that our search for true happiness is to be found in the life of contemplation? Certainly not, if you see contemplation as another solution or even *the* solution to the problems of contemporary life. On the other hand, if you become a contemplative, your problems will probably get themselves solved—though not in the way you expected. For you will begin to see that the "problems" of life only exist because they are inseparably connected with your own illusory exterior self. Most of life's "problems" disappear with the dissolution of this false self.

Yet, if you go the way of contemplation, Merton warns, you must be on guard lest it be your exterior self that turns to contemplation to find "answers" and to achieve fulfillment. The first step toward true contemplation is to renounce this illusory self and to learn that the spiritual self which alone can be contemplative does not seek fulfillment. "It is content to *be* and in its being it is fulfilled, because its being is rooted in God."

Becoming a contemplative does not mean sealing off another compartment of a person's life and telling him that this one is more important than all the rest. On the contrary, the first step toward contemplation is to rid yourself of all compartments and unify your life. You must recover your own natural unity and reintegrate your compartmentalized being into a coordinated and simple whole.

Until we learn to live as unified beings, our lives will be so fragmented that when we say "I" we will not really know who it is that is speaking. It may be an "I" for whom there is no clear "Thou." It may be an "I" that sees other persons simply as extensions of itself. It may be an "I" that sees no clear distinction between itself and other objects. It may be an "I" of projects and temporal finalities that sees in contemplation another project to be accomplished. Such an "I," because its existence is so fragmented, can never become contemplative: for it has lost its own subjectivity.

A person's true subjectivity, his interior "I," has no projects: it seeks to accomplish nothing, not even contemplation. It seeks only to *be* and to move according to the secret dynamics of being itself, following, not its own desires, but the promptings of a superior Freedom. It is this inner self lying dormant in us that must be awakened, if we are to experience the life of contemplation.

The inner self is not something that we can define and then deduce its characteristics from the definition. It is not an object or a thing. It is "not a part of our being, like a motor in a car." It is our entire substantial being itself on its highest, most personal, most existential level. It can only be known as God is known; that is, apophatically. For it is as secret as God Himself and evades every concept by which we try to seize hold of it. It gives depth and reality and a certain incommunicability to every truly spiritual experience. Indeed, every depth experience, whether religious or moral or artistic, is to some extent an experience of the inner self.

Merton sees in the Zen experience of satori an example, on the natural level, of a spiritual enlightenment that reveals the inmost self. For satori is a revolutionary spiritual experience in which, after a long period of purification, there is a kind of inner explosion that blasts the false exterior self to pieces and leaves a person with nothing but his inner self, or, as the Buddhists would say, with nothing but the original face with which one was born. In Buddhist terminology, this experience is the recovery of the "old self" that always existed; for St. Paul, it is the discovery of the new self, or the "new man." This new self that makes its appearance when the false self is dissolved is not an ideal self that we fabricate by our imagination. It is simply ourselves "in all our uniqueness, dignity, littleness and ineffable greatness."

The discovery of the inner self, which the Buddhist experiences in satori, is also the experience of Christian mystics; but with this difference: Zen seems to make no effort to go beyond the inner self, whereas Christian mysticism sees the discovery of the inner self as a stepping-stone to an awareness of God. The Christian mystic passes beyond the inner "I" and "sails into an immense darkness" in which he confronts "the 'I AM' of the Almighty." God reveals Himself interiorly as dwelling in the inmost self.

Merton draws on St. Augustine, the Rhenish mystic John Tauler, and St. John of the Cross to express the Christian experience of the inmost self and the simultaneous awareness of God. The inmost self is the perfect image of God. When it awakens, it finds itself in the presence of Him whose image it is; and by a paradox beyond all human expression, God and the self seem to have but one single "I." They are as though one single person, breathing and living and acting as one. Neither of the "two" is seen as object. There is pure subjectivity beyond all duality.

The inner self stands in a definite relationship to the world of objects, but it has a view of the world radically different from the exterior self. It sees the world, not in bewildering complexity, but in unity. Objects in the external world are not things to be manipulated for pleasure or profit; rather, they are seen with an "immediacy" of vision that does not allow them to become objects of desire or greed or fear. To use a Zen expression, the inner self sees objects "without affirmation or denial." It simply "sees" what it sees.

Merton contrasts a child's vision of a tree with a lumberman's vision. The child sees the tree in a way that is utterly simple and uncolored by ulterior motives. The lumberman, when he sees a tree, may be aware of its beauty but his vision is conditioned by motives of profit and considerations of business. He cannot just "see" the tree.

The inner self also stands in a definite relationship to other subjects. It sees others not as limitations of itself, but as its complement, its other self. Indeed, no one can arrive at a true awareness of his own inner reality, unless he has first become aware of himself as a member of a group; that is, "as an 'I' confronted with a 'thou' that completes and fulfills his own being." The Christian is not merely "alone with the Alone"; he is one with all his brothers and sisters in Christ. His union with them is a unity of love which transcends affirmation of denial. Since the Spirit of Christ dwells in us all, we become, in the mysterious phrase of St. Augustine, "one Christ loving Himself."

This is not to deny that the inner self is the sanctuary of our most personal and individual solitude; it is to say, "what is most personal and solitary in us is what is united with the 'Thou' that confronts us." Without question, a certain withdrawal is necessary in our lives for the perspective that solitude alone can give. But it must be a withdrawal not for the purpose of separation but in the interest of a higher unity. Mere withdrawal without a return to freedom in action can only lead to "a static, death-like inertia of spirit" in which there is no awakening at all.

Real contact with the world of things and with the societal community of men and women is essential for the awakening of the inner self. Equally important is contact with the worshiping community. For all authentic forms of social worship attempt in some manner to provide a religious experience in which the members of the religious group can rise above their individual selves and the group to find themselves and the group at a higher level. This means that all truly serious and spiritual forms of worship aspire at least implicitly to lead their participants to a contemplative awakening of the individual and the group.

But when forms of religious and liturgical worship lose their initial impulse of fervor they tend more and more to forget their contemplative purpose. When the contemplative dimension of worship is lost, one of two things happens: either (1) the participants concentrate on rites and forms for their own sake or for the sake of placating the deity they worship; or (2) they tend to seek an ersatz kind of togetherness at a superficial level that does not allow them to transcend themselves or the group. In either case, the liturgical forms fail in their purpose of enabling the believer to penetrate to his inmost being and serve only to stir up the unconscious emotions of the exterior self. It was against this type of worship that had lost its impulse toward interiority that the Old Testament prophets inveighed. It was this kind of ritual that activates the lips but not the heart that Jesus rebuked in the Pharisees.

The fall described in Genesis was a fall from the unity of the contemplative vision into a condition of multiplicity and distraction and exteriority. Alienated from his inmost spiritual self, the human person was enslaved by an inexorable concern for the exterior, the transient, the illusory, the trivial. No longer able to recognize his own identity in God, he found himself utterly exiled not only from God but also from his own true self. His temptation in this state was "to seek God and happiness outside himself." Thus, his search for God became in fact a flight from God and from his inmost self—a flight that inevitably took him further and further from reality. This state or estrangement in realms of unreality is what is meant by Original Sin.

Our task after the fall is to return to paradise, to recover our lost identity. We have to return to the Father; that is to say, to "that infinite abyss of pure reality" in which alone our own reality is grounded. This return is made possible by the death and resurrection of Jesus Christ, in which we can participate. Our participation consists in a spiritual death in which our exterior self is destroyed and a spiritual resurrection in which our inner self rises from the "dead" by faith and begins to live again in Christ.

Merton sees in the precision of the Nicean and Chalcedon formulation of the mystery of the Incarnation, not simply a theological nicety, but a necessary expression of the central truth of all history.* For it is only in recognizing Christ as the God-man that we can hope once again to achieve our lost union with God. God had to be revealed as human so that all might become One Child of God in Christ.

Because Christ assumed a human nature which is in every respect literally and perfectly human and because that human nature belongs to the Person of the Word of God, everything human in Christ is at the same time divine. The thoughts and actions of Christ are the works of a Divine Person. His very existence is the existence of a Divine Person. In Him we see a Human Being who is in every respect identical with ourselves as far as his human nature is concerned, yet at the same time lives on a completely transcendent divine level of consciousness and being.

By becoming human, Christ makes it possible for us to

---

*Merton's writings seem to show no acquaintance with contemporary Christological formulations.

be divinized. As Athanasius, the great exponent of orthodox Christology, declared, in a formula borrowed from St.
Irenaeus: "God became man in order that man might become God." Christ did not merely reestablish for us a fa-
vorable juridical relation with God; He elevated, changed,
and transformed us into God. Our radical divinization takes
place in baptism; but the divine life remains hidden and
dormant within us until it is more fully developed by a life
of asceticism and charity and, on a higher level, of contemplation.

The Christian renews in his life the self-emptying and
self-transformation by which God became human. "Just as
the Word emptied Himself of His divine and transcendent
nobility in order to 'descend' to the human level, so we
must empty ourselves of what is human in the ignoble sense
of the word, which really means what is less than human,"
in order that we may be raised to the level of God. This
does not mean the destruction of anything that belongs to
human nature as it was assumed by Christ. It does mean "a
radical cutting off of what was not assumed by Him because
it was not capable of being divinized."

This would involve everything that focuses on and per-
petuates our exterior and illusory self to the detriment of
our interior and true self. The inner self is renewed in
Christ and becomes the "new man" of whom St. Paul
speaks. This "new man" is man the contemplative, who
through participation in the Christ-life is assimilated to the
hypostatic union, the union of God and man in Christ. In
Christ we become God's sons and daughters. As St. Paul
says to the Romans (8:6): "The Spirit Himself gives testimony to our spirit that we are the sons [and daughters] of
God." This testimony of the Spirit to our inmost self (i.e.,
our spirit) is what Merton means by Christian contemplation.

THE MIDDLE SECTION OF THE INNER
EXPERIENCE*

In the middle section of *The Inner Experience,* Merton deals
with a variety of material that may perhaps be classified
under the general title of "Kinds of Contemplation," with
particular emphasis on "infused" contemplation. While it
contains some excellent insights on the contemplative life,
this section is the least coordinated part of the book. It
exhibits the "patchwork" characteristic that he spoke of in
his letter to Sister Therese. Sections of *What Is Contemplation,* some of them quite lengthy, are inserted into the text
at various points, and not always harmoniously. Several
ways of handling the subject of contemplation are discussed in the text, but Merton never relates them to one
another. He speaks of the distinction he had made in *What
Is Contemplation* between infused contemplation and active
contemplation, while eschewing the controversy among
theologians of the 1920's and 1930's about the difference
between "acquired" and "infused" contemplation. He
seems to opt for the distinction made by the Greek Fathers
between *natural contemplation (theoria physike)* and *mystical
theology (theologia).* The first is contemplation of God in
nature, not contemplation of the divine by human natural

---

*The middle section of *The Inner Experience* is made up of the following parts:
(a) A chapter on "Kinds of Contemplation" (numbered Chapter IV—the second
chapter to be so labeled). This chapter contains some material from *What Is
Contemplation.* (b) A chapter on "Infused Contemplation" (numbered Chapter
VIII). (c) A section entitled "Five Texts on Contemplation" (obviously a separate
chapter, but given no number). (d) A section entitled "The Paradox of the
Illuminative Way" (obviously a separate chapter, but with no number). (e) A
chapter entitled "What to Do—The Teaching of St. John of the Cross" (numbered Chapter IX). This chapter is taken almost verbatim—but with three addi-
tional paragraphs—from *What Is Contemplation.* (f) A chapter entitled "Some Dangers" (numbered Chapter X and containing material from *What Is Contemplation,*
but with considerable new material added).

powers; the second is contemplation of God as He is in Himself. Yet, after making this distinction and appearing to be quite happy with it, Merton returns once again to the term "infused contemplation," which he discusses in Chapter VII. He corroborates his discussion with an analysis, in an unnumbered chapter, of five texts from well-known mystical writers. In another chapter, which is also unnumbered and which seems to stand by itself, he speaks of "The Paradox of the Illuminative Way" (the awakening and enlightening of the inner self and the darkening and blinding of the exterior self). Then he introduces, somewhat awkwardly, a chapter (numbered Chapter IX) on "What to Do —The Teaching of St. John of the Cross," wherein he turns to the writings of the great Spanish mystic to learn from him how to accept the gift of infused contemplation. Finally, in this section of the book, he deals with some of the dangers that one may encounter in the contemplative way of life (Chapter X, "Some Dangers").

In this middle section of *The Inner Experience,* Merton returns to a discussion of the kinds of contemplation that he had developed in *What Is Contemplation;* namely, passive and active contemplation.

Passive contemplation is the passive intuition of our inmost self and of God. It is an understanding of contemplation that is primarily theological; for it is not empirically verifiable, being known to us only as a datum of revelation. Christ's words in St. John's Gospel that He will "manifest Himself" to those who love him suggests a divine activity which the one who contemplates is in no position to bring about by his own efforts. In the classical mystical expression, such a grace is effected "in us and without us" *(in nobis et sine nobis).* Active or meditative contemplation, on the other hand, is effected in us, but with our cooperation *(in nobis et non sine nobis).* Passive contemplation involves no conceptual mediation: it is without concepts and images. It is essentially apophatic. Active contemplation uses concepts and judgments and acts of faith. It may be a springboard for moments of contemplative intuition.

Active contemplation is the deliberate and sustained effort to discover the will of God in the events of life and to bring one's whole being into harmony with the divine will. This involves three things. (1) It means being in touch with the logos of the age; namely, "having an intuitive grasp and even empathy for what is most genuine in the movements of the day" (e.g., movements in our day such as Marxism, existentialism, psychoanalysis). (2) It means being in touch with our own inner life, directing that life according to one's inner truth and striving for unity in that life nourished by meditation, reading, and the liturgical life of the Church. (3) It means confronting reality with a sense of awe. (It is this sense of awe and reverence that distinguishes active contemplation from a kind of aesthetic contemplation that rests in the beauty of abstract truth.)

Liturgy is "the ordinary focus of active contemplation." For, in the liturgy, one enters into the Church's contemplation of the great mysteries of faith. Liturgies of the Word, announcing the Gospel (the kerygma), put us in touch with the mystery of salvation. As we hear the Word of salvation, it enters the depths of our being and awakens anew in us our divine life as sons and daughters of God. Eucharistic liturgies unite the Christian sacramentally with the Risen Lord; for they symbolize and effect the mystical union of the believer with Christ in love.

Active contemplation also means union with God in the activities of one's life. This is the normal way to contemplation for the great majority of Christians. They are "hidden contemplatives."* They abandon themselves to the will of God and keep in touch with the realities of the present moment; that is to say, the inner and spiritual realities, not the surface emotions and excitements which in reality are nothing but illusion. They swim with the living stream of life, remaining in contact with God in the hiddenness and ordinariness of the present moment and the tasks it brings. In this way, ordinary activities—such as walking down a street, sweeping a floor, taking a stroll in the woods—can be enriched with a contemplative sense of the presence of God. Being in touch with God in this way is "one of the simplest and most secure ways of living a life of prayer— and one of the safest." Those who follow this way may achieve a high degree of sanctity—even greater perhaps than that of those who are "juridically" called to live lives of contemplation.

Choosing to ignore the controversy about the differences between "acquired" and "infused" contemplation—a controversy engendered in an earlier generation by such theologians as Garrigou-Lagrange—Merton turns to the Greek Fathers and accepts the distinction they drew between natural contemplation *(theoria physike)* and mystical theology *(theologia)*.

Natural contemplation is "the intuition of divine things in and through the reflections of God in nature and in the symbols of revelation." Such contemplation presupposes a long ascetic preparation that delivers one from attachment to exterior things and produces a purity of heart and a singleness of view that enables one to see straight into the nature of things as they are. "Natural" contemplation is

---

*The reader will note that Merton is here reworking material from *What Is Contemplation,* where he speaks of those who are united with God in activity as "quasi-contemplatives." See Chapter I.

natural, not in its origin, but in its object: it is "the contemplation of the divine in *nature,* not contemplation of the divine by our *natural powers*." Such contemplation, while it implies ascetic preparation on the part of the contemplative, is mystical in that it is God's gift of enlightenment, enabling us really to see the created world as it is and to see the symbols of God's presence with which it is filled.

Theologia, or pure contemplation, is "the direct quasi-experimental contact with God beyond all thought, that is, without the medium of concepts." Since it brooks no medium between God and our inmost spirit, it is in this sense direct contact with God. Such direct contact with God is not a matter of spiritual effort or intellectual learning. It is an identification with God by love, for it is love that constitutes in us the likeness of God. At the same time, it is a meeting with God in the darkness of unknowing. This embrace in darkness is absolutely essential to pure contemplation, because, with the elimination of concepts and images, all natural lights are put out. One knows God through his "own divinized subjectivity." St. Gregory of Nyssa aptly compares the mystic to Moses ascending Mt. Sinai and entering into the dark cloud where he is face to face with God. The inmost self ascends into the darkness with no concepts at all. Then he can touch, or rather be touched by, God. In the cloud of unknowing, "the gap between our spirit as subject and God as object is finally closed and in the embrace of mystical love we know that we and He are one."

But the cloud into which we enter has not only a light shining in the darkness; it has also a fire that wages a relentless attack against the last vestiges of self-love that remain in us. There are times when this fire strips us of all the consolations we once enjoyed in prayer, and we are left in a state of terrible inward anguish in which we seem no longer able to pray or to love. This anguish may at times be accentuated when conflicts arise between the inward light of God, however dimly perceived, and the outward claims made on our obedience by the community in which we live. Such conflicts are not unlikely, since the call into the darkness is a call to leave familiar and conventional patterns of thought and action.

In the midst of this anguish and these conflicts, we must come to realize that God is drawing us to a deeper emptying of all that is incompatible with His love. We become indifferent to ourselves and even to our spiritual ambitions. Knowing that we are one with God in love, we gradually cease to worry about ourselves and about useless questions. We learn to leave "all decisions to God in the wordlessness of a present that knows no explanations, no projects and no plans." As Eckhart says: mystical love of God is a "love that asks no questions."

In an unnumbered chapter called "Five Texts on Contemplation," Merton wrestles with the question of what it means to be in the cloud of unknowing; that is, what it means to know without "knowing." He asks whether this "knowledge" admits of doubt. On the conceptual level, it certainly does, for in terms of logic it appears to be irrational. But on another level, the level of immediate intuition, there is no doubt; one knows without ambiguity. It is a knowledge that is akin to our experience of our own being, which we know without doubt.

The texts* he quotes to show that knowing beyond concepts and images is real "knowledge" are, paradoxically, texts that have recourse to rich metaphorical language to express the directness and the reality of the experience of God in contemplative prayer. But reading between the

---

*The texts are taken from (1) St. John of the Cross; (2) Blessed John Ruysbroeck; (3) *The Cloud of Unknowing;* (4) Meister Eckhart; and (5) St. Bernard of Clairvaux.

lines of these texts makes it clear that they are speaking of contemplation as an intuition that is deep, dynamic, and loving, yet beyond all comparison with the mere conceptual grasp which is ours on the ordinary level of experience. While they use the language of images, they are quick to point out that no amount of imagination and metaphor can begin to convey what is meant by the contemplative experience of God's presence in the soul.

In the early stages of the contemplative life, "there is a kind of preexperimental contemplation in which the self plunges into the darkness without knowing why and tends toward something it knows not." But as one progresses in contemplation there is a strong subjective verification of the truth that this "something" toward which the soul is groping is more than an idea of God or a desire for His presence: it is God Himself.

When one feels that he is moving toward infused contemplation, two questions arise: (1) How can he know that he has really entered into the state of infused contemplation, especially when that state seems to be accompanied by a sense of aridity and apparent irrationality? and: (2) What ought he to do in this situation?

Merton answers these two questions in the last section of "Five Texts" and in Chapter IX, "What to Do—The Teaching of St. John of the Cross." The answers are drawn almost verbatim from *What Is Contemplation.* For the answers to these questions, therefore, the reader is referred to Chapter I of this book, pages 25–30, where this material from *What Is Contemplation* is discussed.

In the midst of this material—namely, between the chapter entitled "Five Texts on Contemplation" and Chapter IX, entitled "What to Do—The Teaching of St. John of the Cross"—Merton has inserted, rather awkwardly, an entirely new chapter (unnumbered) called "The Paradox of the Illuminative Way." This chapter, while it does not seem to fit the context, does nonetheless offer valuable insights.

The discovery of God in the inmost depths of our being, Merton says, marks a "shift from the exterior life to an interior life in the strict sense of the word." For, while the term "interior life" can be a valid description of a life that strives for prayer and self-discipline, the interior life properly so called actually comes alive only when "this inner and spiritual consciousness has been awakened."

The paradox of the illuminative way, therefore, always involves a darkening and blinding of the exterior self and an awakening and enlightening of the inner self. At this point it is necessary to darken and put to sleep the discursive and rational lights that one was familiar with in meditation. This is no easy task and can be done only with the help of God's grace. For one tends to feel guilty about relaxing and resting in the darkness; and there is a strong inclination to climb back into the safety and security of the boat of habit and convention.

In a striking analogy Merton compares this critical point in the life of a contemplative to the battle of Jacob with the angel. "It is the battle of our own strength, lodged in the exterior self, with the strength of God, which is the life and actuality of our inner self." It is a battle that takes place in the darkness. The angel, our inner self, wounds a nerve in our thigh, so that ever afterwards we limp; that is to say, our natural powers are crippled. Though we do not overcome our antagonist, yet we do not let him go till he blesses us. And when we are blessed, we receive a new name, Israel, which means "He who sees God." And this new name makes us contemplatives. But when we ask the name of our antagonist, no answer is given us, for our inmost self is unknown, just as God Himself is unknown.

St. John of the Cross defines this battle in terms of twofold purification: (1) the dark night of the senses, which is a purification of the exterior and interior senses that brings one to the threshold of contemplation; and (2) the dark night of the spirit, in which even the interior self is purified. "In the first night the exterior man 'dies' to rise and become the inner man; in the second night the interior man dies and rises so completely united to God that the two are one." It is "as if the soul itself were God and God were the soul." In the words of St. John of the Cross, the soul is completely lost in God, "as a drop of water in a flagon of pure wine."

In the last chapter of what I have called the middle section of *The Inner Experience,* Merton warns against certain experiences which bear a resemblance to, or have an affinity with, contemplation but which in fact are the complete contradiction of it. Specifically he speaks of the dangers of (1) quietism; (2) nonreligious existentialism; and (3) illuminism.*

The quietist seeks, like the contemplative, to "empty" himself. But whereas "the contemplative empties his heart of every created love to be filled with the love of God and divests his mind of all created images to receive the pure and simple light of God directly into the summit of his soul," the quietist empties himself of *all* love and *all* knowledge and remains inert in a vacuum, where there is no passive receptivity, but only a blank without light or warmth or breath of interior life. The contemplative seeks to deepen love and to perfect all the virtues in that contemplative love. The quietist, on the other hand, sees the quest for virtue as "self-love"and the desire to practice virtue and avoid sin as "imperfections" that trouble the "peace" of

---

*The danger of quietism is discussed in *What Is Contemplation.* Merton's treatment of it in *The Inner Experience* is largely borrowed from the earlier work.

the "annihilated" soul. The quietist remains inactive with no desire at all, not even the desire of God. The contemplative sometimes suffers from the fact that he thinks he is without the desire for God. The contemplative may at times find himself in a condition of loneliness and isolation and anguished waiting upon God in the darkness. Yet his inarticulate longing for God in the night of suffering may well be his most eloquent prayer. If he continues to seek God in love and self-abasement, he will find God; and he will know that he has not fallen victim to quietism.

The contemplative who is inclined to take too philosophically the inevitable emptiness of life "finds himself in the same territory as the existentialist." In fact, the nonreligious existentialist may find the dark night of the spirit an aspect of Christian mysticism that appeals to him. He is able to identify with the lonely figure of the solitary believer committing himself to a heroic risk and "staking everything on his decision to walk in the darkness beyond all concepts, hoping he will find the Ultimate Reality which concepts are inadequate to describe." The existentialist may see in such a figure a counterpart of himself accepting an "absurd" freedom in an "absurd" universe. Yet the difference between the two is very great. It is one thing to accept one's own absolute autonomy in a world of absurdity; it is quite another thing to accept "the transcendent Divine Reality behind the apparent absurdity of everyday life." There is a huge difference between a person who is "shut up in himself and cannot open his heart to another being and the man who has forgotten himself and becomes lost in Being."

This is not to say that there are no bonds between the contemplative and the existentialist. Existentialism is an ambiguous term. It has popularly been identified with Jean-Paul Sartre, who is an atheist. But there are also existentialists who are men of deep religious commitment, such as Sören Kierkegaard, Gabriel Marcel, Nicholas Berdyaev, Paul Tillich. Paul Tillich, an existentialist, defined faith as "ultimate concern."

> What unites contemplatives and existentialists is precisely the depth and sincerity of their "concern." Both reject any easy or convenient substitute for ultimate reality. Both face the insecurity and darkness of spiritual risk.

For these reasons, dialogue is possible between them.

A third danger faced by the contemplative is the danger of "illuminism," or what Ronald Knox called "enthusiasm." Illuminism consists in taking one's subjective experience so seriously that it becomes more important than God. Spiritual experience, sought for its own sake, is objectified and turned into an idol. It becomes an "object," a "thing" that we serve. The contemplative must realize that he was "not created for the service of any 'thing,' but for the service of God who is not and cannot be a 'thing.' To serve Him who is no 'object' is freedom." To live for any "thing," whether it be something base (such as money, pleasure, or success) or something spiritual (such as a religious experience), is to be enslaved. Attaching exclusive importance to what we "experience" in prayer is to wander from the true path of contemplation.

A true contemplative is no sensationalist: he loves sobriety and obscurity. Having no taste for spiritual excitement, being content to remain at peace in emptiness without projects and vanities, he is delivered from subjection to appearances. And should he be considered a fool, he is quite content. For he stands in a long line of mystics going back to Paul of Tarsus, who was glad to be considered "a fool for the sake of Christ."

THE LAST SECTION OF THE INNER EXPERIENCE*

The first section of *The Inner Experience* deals with the question who the contemplative is. Merton's answer is that the true self, fully awakened, attuned to solitude, yet in touch with the real world of objects and persons, alone can be the subject of contemplation. The middle section attempts to answer the questions what contemplation is and how to deal with the experience of it. Merton draws on patristic and mystical literature to formulate his answers. The last section discusses a number of different topics which may be linked together under the general title of the concomitants of contemplation in the contemporary world. The following topics are covered: (1) Contemplation and Neurosis (Chapter XI); (2) The Desire of Contemplation (Chapter XII); (3) The Sense of Sin (Chapter XIII); (4) Problems of the Contemplative Life (Chapter XIV); and (5) Prospects and Conclusions (Chapter XV).

In a world that senses a deep emptiness at the heart of human life, there exists the possibility of a neurotic approach to interiority that can produce a kind of pseudo-mysticism. Withdrawal, as Merton points out more than once, is a necessary feature of the contemplative life. Yet the word "withdrawal" is an ambiguous term. For there is a kind of withdrawal that is harmful to the human spirit. When we speak of a person who is "withdrawn," we generally use the word in a pejorative sense: it indicates withdrawal from involvement in human life to seek escape in a false interiority that becomes a prison. There is also a right kind of withdrawal that seeks solitude and silence in order to face the demands of life with our heads and hearts to-

---

*Pages 104–50, including Chapters XI–XV. This section contains no material from *What Is Contemplation.*

gether. The first kind of withdrawal is neurotic; the second may be contemplative.

The contemplative withdraws into solitude, not to evade reality, but to find things and accept them as they are. The neurotic withdraws not so much into solitude as into the empty shell of his own inwardness to enjoy "the false sweetness of a narcissistic seclusion." The contemplative sees reality as it is; the neurotic accepts only as much reality as he can bear, shutting out the rest. The contemplative enters into his nothingness and finds peace and relaxation, for he finds God there and experiences himself as a free person. The neurotic enters into his nothingness and finds only anxiety and tension, for his concern is not with God but with himself. The contemplative thinks not of himself; the neurotic thinks only of himself.* The contemplative prays with the hope of experiencing God; the neurotic prays with the hope of achieving reassurance that will "allay his anxieties and justify his withdrawal from reality as a religious act." The contemplative trusts in God and therefore is at peace; the neurotic trusts only in himself and therefore is always in turmoil.

Because there are superficial similarities between the contemplative and the neurotic, it may happen that an apparent contemplative disposition may actually mask an unhealthy neurosis that is unwilling to face the reality of human life. Indeed, this may well be a particular phenomenon of an age like ours that is obsessed with the emptiness of human life. The temptation is strong to squeeze whatever bit of meaning we can get out of our solitary selves and to ignore any meaning outside us or beyond us.

---

*Merton points to the deep symbolic meaning the Fathers found in the Genesis story of the fall. The forbidden tree in the garden is the tree of self which we are not supposed to see or notice. When we take notice of it, we are divided within ourselves and alienated from external reality.

Sometimes the security and regularity of the monastic life can create an atmosphere that is quite comfortable to the neurotic. For he can hope to find in a scrupulous and exact observance of the rules the reassurance that allays his anxieties, without requiring any true encounter with the realities of life as they are.

Contemplation is an awareness of what cannot be experienced in this life. It is knowing God as unknown and by unknowing, "an apophatic grasp of Him Who is." As such, it cannot be satisfactorily explained to one who has not had the experience; at the same time, one who has had it can recognize it in others. This is because contemplation is a common religious phenomenon that is not limited to any age or place or society. Whether it is thought of as natural or supernatural, it is an experience that is possible for anyone who sincerely seeks the truth and responds to God's grace. That is why anyone can desire it.

Yet he who would desire it must renounce all preconceived notions about what it is and open himself to a completely new experience. Moreover, he must put aside all ambition to achieve it. One can only desire it by "not desiring" it. Anyone who thinks of contemplation as something lofty and spectacular that he seeks to accomplish cannot receive the intuition of that Reality that is at once transcendent and at the same time immanent in his ordinary self.

A person who knows that he does not know and who opens himself to the truth without pride in his own capacities and without personal ambition may indeed experience the desire for contemplative freedom arising in himself unobserved. Then he is on the road to contemplation, because, paradoxically, he knows that there is no such road.

To take the first step toward contemplative freedom one needs not so much an awareness of what lies at the end of the road—namely, the experience of God—as a clear view of the obstacle that blocks the road at the very beginning; namely, the obstacle of sin. This is especially necessary today, for our age has lost the sense of sin and replaced it with a sense of guilt. A sense of sin can be a productive experience, leading to conversion of spirit. A sense of guilt, on the other hand, can actually deaden our realization of the meaning of sin in our lives.

Guilt is a kind of prurient feeling of naughtiness for having violated the taboos of one's religion. It is a sense of oppression from the outside: an experience of anxiety in which one feels that he is going to be called to account for a misdeed. I experience guilt when I think that someone else believes me to be in the wrong.

Guilt can be dealt with in two ways: (1) by gestures of piety that symbolize good intentions and therefore assuage conscience and obscure the sense of sin; or (2) by transferring guilt to the group and thereby escaping personal responsibility. This tendency to make sin a collective responsibility rather than a personal one is very strong in our day. The more collective responsibility becomes, the more nebulous it is. Then the most terrible crimes can be accepted without a tremor, because the guilt is "theirs," not "mine." Witness the willingness of the majority of "believers" to accept the hydrogen bomb with all its implications, and with scarcely a murmur of protest. Sin is something much deeper and more existential than guilt.

> It is a sense of evil in myself not because I have violated a law outside myself, but because I have violated the inmost laws of my own being which are, at the same time, the laws of God who dwells in me.

The sense of sin is the sense of "being deeply and deliberately false to my inmost being and therefore to my likeness to God." It is a sense of inner falsity which tells me not merely that I have *done* wrong but that I *am* wrong.

"The mission of the contemplative is to keep alive in the world the sense of sin," and to nurture, at least in himself, a sense of personal responsibility before God and a personal independence from collective irresponsibility. In fulfilling this mission, the contemplative is the descendant of the Old Testament prophets; for it was their mission to confront the people of Israel with the reality of sin, which cut them off from God, and to make them distinguish sin from ritual guilt, which could be set right with legal ceremonies. The prophets did not preach an abstract morality: they called people to accept the concrete will of God.

The contemplative, like the prophet, is aware not only of his own sins but of the sins of the world, which he takes upon himself, because he is a person of his own times and cannot dissociate himself from the deeds of other people. In an age that has known Auschwitz and Dachau, our contemplation is something darker and more fearsome than the contemplation of the Church Fathers. For it must embody a deep sorrow and a healing, life-giving repentance for the mystery of evil that stands as a wall between us and God. Contemplation that would shrink from the burden of our days and refuse to share the misery of others would only be an escape into unreality and spiritual illusion.

Our age, perhaps more than any other, has experienced the absence of God. Indeed, in some circles it has proclaimed that God is dead. In such an age, God must often seem to be "absent" from our contemplation. The truth is that never more than today God makes His presence felt by "being absent." Our contemplation, therefore, need not be a vain struggle to try to make Him present, but rather an acceptance of apparent emptiness and absence, while we realize, if only dimly, that in the nothingness that seems to engulf us He is more surely present.

In discussing the practical problems that men and women encounter in their efforts to live a contemplative life in today's world, Merton develops a theme that is familiar to those who have read his books of social criticism; namely, that the technological society we live in and the television culture it has engendered have all but destroyed our natural disposition to contemplation. In pre-industrial ages—and this is true of primitive societies that still exist —one was formed by his tradition and culture; and even though he might not be able to read or write, he possessed a fund of important and vital knowledge that was integrated into his life. He had a wholesome simplicity and a healthy self-confidence which prepared him for and disposed him toward the contemplative experience. The technological orientation of contemporary society, with its tendency to manipulate persons and cast them into a single mold, beclouds the natural and spontaneous signs of spirituality. Imagination, originality, and freshness of response to reality that tended to characterize pre-industrial societies have been replaced, in our technological world, by fears and anxieties and the compulsion to conform that assail contemporary men and women from all sides. The result is that the disposition to contemplation that was once natural to the human person has to be recovered and learned. This is a difficult task not only in the "world" but also in the monastery.

Where can a person find the proper setting where in silence and detachment he can learn the ways of the interior life? The most obvious answer is a monastic or contemplative community. The monastery provides a way of life that is supposed to be oriented toward contemplation. It is a place where you find yourself living among contemplatives and where spiritual direction is readily available. Indeed, the community life of the monastery is a kind of "sacrament" of the presence of God. This at least is the ideal expressed in the Rule of St. Benedict—a Rule which through the centuries has proved itself adaptable to new situations and which offers a wholesome combination of liturgy, labor, study, and contemplation.

In practice, however, there is often a gap between the ideal and the real situation that exists. A monastery is a community of "juridical" contemplatives—that is, a community of men whose way of life involves a commitment to contemplation—but, in actual fact, there are all too many monasteries that "contain few or no real contemplatives." The rigidly institutional character of monastic life today can inhibit contemplative development. The factory-like atmosphere of very large monasteries requires so many jobs to be done that the things that are most necessary tend to be forgotten. Though the monastic life is based, in theory, on a medieval pattern, the tempo is often that of a modern place of business, with none of the seemingly aimless leisure and thoughtlessness of time that the contemplative spirit requires. The monastery has not remained immune from the influences of technology.

It is true that there has been a large influx of vocations to the monastic life and that new types of monasteries have come into existence; nonetheless, anyone who expects the monks to carry the torch of culture through a new dark age is, Merton says, due for disappointment.*

Indeed, the influx of large numbers of hopeful candi-

---

*This represents a drastic departure from the enthusiastic *apologia* for the monastic life that is found in *Seven Storey Mountain* and in *The Secular Journal*. Because of the renewal of monastic life that began in the 1960's under the influence of the Second Vatican Council—a renewal in which his own writings played a significant role—Merton's later writings present a more hopeful and optimistic picture of the meaning of the monastic life for the contemporary world. See his essays in *Contemplation in a World of Action* and *The Monastic Journey;* also his talks in *The Asian Journal.*

dates presenting themselves at the monastic gate creates its own set of problems. There is nothing in the monastic rule, Merton points out, to prepare the monastery for the arrival of the television addict. It cannot be taken for granted that young postulants who seek admission to the monastery really know their own minds or have their lives together. Most often, they are immature and lack the background of a true liberal education. They may have gone through a process of education, but much of it had little to do with real life. It may have taught them ways to control things and to manipulate persons, but not how to be free from external compulsions and how to open themselves to their own inner truth. They are formless bundles of unrelated factual knowledge that is largely superficial and not integrated into their lives. They do not really "know" what they know, for what they have "learned" has not been personally appropriated by them. Their lives are often a pitiful mixture of pseudo-sophistication and utter vacuity.

Moreover, the television culture, in which they have been indoctrinated, encourages passivity and receptivity, but unfortunately of the wrong kind. Certainly, the passivity and receptivity that are the fruits of an active and intransigent struggle with all that captivates and enslaves the senses and the emotions and the will are qualities essential to contemplation; but they are not conducive to contemplation if they are the result of the inertia and uncritical absorption of material and temporal "values" poured out of a television machine. Young candidates who are formed (or deformed) by such a culture are not unprepared simply for the contemplative life; they are unprepared for any kind of human life.

If monasteries are going to accept such undeveloped candidates, there is need, before ever they enter the novitiate, for separate communities of postulants. Here they can be given not only an elementary religious formation but also the opportunities for normal human experience, in which, one would hope, they will be able to find a certain amount of depth in their lives and come to appreciate the value of silence and of being along with themselves.

Such things, Merton believes, cannot be done in a novitiate. You cannot teach asceticism to someone who has not had, in any depth, truly human experiences. You cannot speak of "mortification" of the senses to someone who has never had the pleasure of using his senses normally and innocently in the enjoyment of the good things of nature. Only one who has learned to *see* with his own eyes and *taste* with his own tongue and *experience* reality with his whole being can ever begin to understand the meaning of ascetical discipline.

St. Theresa of Avila, in Chapter VI of the *Book of Foundations,* counsels those who have been led into exaggerations and delusions in their prayer life to distract themselves deliberately from what they think to be spiritual, in order "to keep in touch with ordinary human realities of life." A person has to be attuned to what is truly human before he can be ascetical—or contemplative.

The cloistered monk in his contemplative quest has the support of an institutional structure geared to contemplation. He has also an atmosphere of solitude that protects him in part at least from the pressures and distractions of secular life. The lay person, intent on an interior life, has neither the structure nor the atmosphere conducive to the spiritual quest. If he wishes to enjoy even an elementary life of prayer, he must be willing to face the ceaseless struggle to keep himself free from the collective pressures that subject him to the spirit of the world and deaden his sensitivity to the spirit of God. This struggle involves two things. First, it means reducing the conflicts in his life by cutting down contacts with the world and subjection to secular concerns. This requires reducing the need for pleasure, comfort, prestige, and success and embracing a life of relative poverty and detachment. Second, it means putting up with the conflicts that remain: the noise, the agitation, the lack of time, the constant contact with a secular mentality which seems to engulf us on all sides and from which we can never be wholly delivered.

Lay people should seek some kind of structure, however informal, that will join them with others of similar intent, perhaps with the help of a priest who is truly interested in contemplation, and possibly in contact with a contemplative community. (Merton envisions the possibility of a contemplative Third Order attached to a Cistercian or Carthusian monastery.) Such a group of lay people could provide its members with books, conferences, spiritual direction, perhaps even a quiet spot in the country to go to for brief periods of prayer and solitude.

Structure is not enough; there is also the need of creating the atmosphere of quiet and solitude so essential to spiritual growth. Merton offers three suggestions toward this goal:

1. Lay people interested in the interior life should seek a place to live and an occupation to engage in that will offer them opportunities for solitude. Even though it might entail some economic sacrifice, they might move to the country or to a small town, where they would have more opportunity to think and to get their lives together. The relative poverty that such a move might involve would liberate them from the pitiless struggle to keep their standards of life at the level of the rest of society. As regards occupation, probably not everyone is ready to embrace the life of a forest ranger or a lighthouse keeper or a night watchman, but, Merton asks, what is wrong with farming?

2. They might rearrange the schedule of their daily activities so as to enjoy those parts of the day which are quiet because the world does not value them. The early hours of the morning, when most people are asleep, offer you the opportunity of having the whole world to yourself so that you can taste the peace of solitude. Dawn is a peaceful, mysterious contemplative time of the day—a time that speaks of new life and new beginnings. It is well suited to symbolize the continual interior spiritual renewal that must characterize our life in Christ.

3. They should make special efforts to keep Sunday as a day of contemplation. Sunday is sacred to the mystery of the Resurrection. It is a time to contemplate all that God has done for us, and especially what He has done in Christ. It is not, therefore, just a pause in the week, but a burst of light out of a sacred eternity entering into the otherwise ceaseless round of secular time.

> We should stop working and rushing around on Sunday, not just to rest so that we can start over again on Monday, but to collect our wits and to realize the relative meaninglessness of the secular business that fills the other six days of the week.

On Sunday we can taste the satisfaction of the peace that only Christ can give—a peace which, if we orient our work toward it, can filter through the rest of the week.

A lay person intent on living an interior life must not attempt to be a monk in the world. His prayer life cannot be pure contemplation; he must be content to be what Merton calls a "masked contemplative." For active virtue and good works must necessarily play a large part in his "contemplative" life. He must be faithful to the duties of his state in life, whether as head of a family, member of a profession, or citizen of his country. Married Christians must see their contemplation linked closely with their married life. Indeed, their expression of married love is a symbol of the human desire for God and for oneness with Him. The Greek Fathers believed that, before the fall, Adam and Eve were literally one flesh, one single being. The fall divided them into two, and ever after, sexual love has been an effort to recover that lost unity. Yet perfect unity cannot be realized by man and woman. It can be realized only in Christ who has married human nature and united it to God in His own Person. Sexual union is a symbol, however frail and incomplete, of that perfect union of humanity with God effected in the Incarnation. Since the love of married Christians mirrors, though dimly and incompletely, the perfection of Christian love, their contemplative spirituality must be rooted and centered in the mystery of Christian marriage.

In the final pages of *The Inner Experience,* Merton discusses the future of the contemplative life in the contemporary world. Contemplation today, he insists, cannot consist merely in withdrawal into a subjective peace that evades responsibility for the world, of which the contemplative, like everyone else, is after all a part. The contemplative must learn in his withdrawal the unique contribution he can make to that world.

What this contribution is to be can perhaps be learned by studying two significant twentieth-century innovations in contemplative living; namely, the Fraternities of the Little Brothers of Jesus, and the Indian experiment of the late Father Monchanin.

The Little Brothers of Jesus are small groups of men who live in every respect like the lay people around them, except that they dedicate themselves to God and focus their lives on a contemplative center. They are not a religious order: they wear no habit; they have no enclosed monasteries. In imitation of Jesus of Nazareth, they live and work among the poor, dwelling in the same kind of homes as the poor, accepting the kinds of jobs that are open to the poor. The one thing that distinguishes them from other workers in their area is the fact that in their homes there is an altar and a tabernacle of the Blessed Sacrament. Their home altar is the center of their contemplative life and they spend much of their free time before the tabernacle. As they live the lives of the poor, so their prayer is the prayer of the poor —subject to distraction, fatigue, incapacity to meditate, and even apparent failure.

They have no special pastoral task: they do not try to convert people or to get them to amend their lives. They seek only to *be* with them, sharing their lives, their poverty, their suffering, their hopes. Their life is one of utter simplicity, reflecting the simplicity of the Gospel. Though they are "masked contemplatives" (for they have not the luxury of the solitude that pure contemplation requires), their way of living represents a strictly contemplative view of life. For the people among whom they live, they are a burning symbol of the presence of Christ in their midst.

The ideal of the Little Brothers was discovered and lived at the beginning of the twentieth century by Charles de Foucauld, a onetime army officer converted from a worldly life, who entered a Trappist monastery, then left it to live in the Sahara Desert. He lived among the Tuaregs, whom he selected as the poorest and most abandoned of people. He studied their language and tried to help them economically and spiritually.

His formula for the contemplative life was—and perhaps still is—an enigma to those who link contemplation with separation from the world, silence, and monastic enclosure. Yet is it not true, Merton asks, that this man who withdrew from a well-to-do and highly sophisticated society to live among a poor and primitive people in the middle of the desert had "left the world" more truly and completely than the person who, remaining in his civilized society, enters one of its wealthy, comfortable, mechanized, highly respected monasteries? Charles de Foucauld was not unlike the early Desert Fathers, those pioneers of the contemplative life, who were laymen like the Tuaregs and who lived in the desert in Egypt much the same kind of life that Charles de Foucauld lived in the Sahara.

A second contemplative innovation of the twentieth century was that of Father Monchanin, a French secular priest, who attempted to bring the Christian contemplative tradition in contact with the mysticism of the East. He went with a companion to South India, where he formed an ashram, a monastery of simple huts, without chairs or tables or European furniture. He went there not to extend the Christian contemplative life to a "pagan" country but to study Hindu mysticism. Like the great saints of the past who incorporated into Christianity what was good in Greek philosophy, he sought to discover whatever might be germane to the Gospel in the rich store of Eastern mysticism.*

These two examples of innovation in contemplative living—the Little Brothers seeing the world as their "cloister," and Father Monchanin seeking to form Christian links with the mysticism of the East—can shed light on the deepest meaning of the contemplative and monastic life in the contemporary world.

---

*His experiment was a far cry from that of the contemplative monasteries that went into "mission lands" in the nineteenth century and, in blatantly "colonial" fashion, become "branch offices" of the European motherhouses, the monks living in a culture that they neither understood nor cared to understand and making pseudo-Europeans of candidates who applied for entrance to their monasteries. Though they may have produced some fruits, these monasteries were doomed to extinction once the colonial powers were driven out of the country.

A contemplative is not just a person who separates himself from others and goes off to meditate while they struggle to make a living. He does not forget the world and its struggles in order to sit absorbed in prayer, "while bombers swarm in the air over his monastery." The contemplative is one who lives a life that tends toward unity. True, he must begin by separating himself from the ordinary activities of other people so that in recollection and solitude he can find the inner center of his life, which remains inaccessible as long as he is immersed in an exterior life.

But contemplation is not intended to be a life of permanent withdrawal into oneself. The contemplative is not one who is less interested than others in what is going on in the world; if anything, he should be more interested—precisely because he is a contemplative. Indeed, he should not only be more interested in what happens, he should be more perceptive of the real issues at stake. For if he has achieved true purity of heart, he is less likely to be involved in the surface confusion that most people take for reality. He will have a more spiritual grasp of what is "real" and "actual," a deeper appreciation of values that are permanent, human, and truly spiritual.

His contribution to the world will not be that of the specialist, skilled in political science or economics or any other particular discipline, but that of the person who is whole and unified in his own being and who seeks to communicate an intuition of wholeness and unity to others. Because he is in touch with what is most deeply real, he is attuned to the logos of his own time, with a compassion for people's deepest sufferings and a sensitivity to their most viable hopes. He has a mystique of history: a contemplative view of a humanity moving toward that final unity of all things at the *parousia* of the Lord, a unity which he must not simply anticipate passively but must help to bring about by the action of his own creative freedom. He is humble enough not to engage in a promethean struggle to divinize himself by his own techniques and powers; he is wise enough to realize that "the free cooperation of his creative love with the love of God will lead him to fulfill his true call to divinity as a child of God."

Above all else, the contemplative can offer an insight into human freedom to his contemporaries who seek emancipation and liberty but whose tragedy is that they seek it in the wrong way and by means that lead only to deeper enslavement. The contemplative can teach the world that freedom is rooted, not in us, but in God. We can be free only when we participate in the freedom of God. To be free is to renounce the struggle to dominate others and the slavery of being dominated by our own desires. Freedom means liberation from our false, manipulative self in order to discover our true and free self in God. Then, like Adam in Paradise before the fall, we can walk as free persons with our God in the cool of the evening breeze.

V

The Inner Experience:
*Selected Texts** *

One of the strange laws of the contemplative life is that in it you do not sit down and solve problems: you bear with them until they somehow solve themselves. Or until life itself solves them for you. Usually the solution consists in a discovery that they exist only insofar as they were inseparably connected with your own illusory exterior self. The solution of most such problems comes with the dissolution of this false self. And consequently another law of the contemplative life is that if you enter it with the set purpose of seeking contemplation, or, worse still, happiness, you will find neither. For neither can be found unless it is first in some sense renounced. And again, this means renouncing the illusory self that seeks to be "happy," and to find "fulfillment" (whatever that may mean) in contemplation. For the contemplative and spiritual self, the dormant, mys-

*The texts in this chapter are taken from the fourth draft of *The Inner Experience.* The titles of the chapters of *The Inner Experience,* together with the pages covered in each chapter, may be found in the diagram on pages 78–79.

terious, and hidden self that is always effaced by the activity of our exterior self, does not seek fulfillment. It is content to be, and in its being it is fulfilled, because its being is rooted in God. [p. 2]

The worst thing that can happen to a man who is already divided up into a dozen different compartments is to seal off yet another compartment and tell him that this one is more important than all the others . . .

The first thing you have to do, before you even start thinking about such a thing as contemplation, is to try to recover your basic natural unity, to reintegrate your compartmentalized being into a coordinated and simple whole, and learn to live as a unified human person. This means that you have to bring back together the fragments of your distracted existence, so that when you say "I," there is really someone present to support the pronoun you have uttered. [p. 3]

Reflect, sometimes, on the disquieting fact that most of your statements of opinions, tastes, deeds, desires, hopes, and fears are statements about someone who is not really present. When you say, "I think," it is often not you who think, but "they"—it is the anonymous authority of the collectivity speaking through your mask. When you say "I want," you are sometimes simply making an automatic gesture of accepting, paying for, what has been forced upon you. That is to say, you reach out for what you have been made to want . . .

This, however, is not the "I" who can stand in the presence of God and be aware of Him as a "Thou." For this "I," there is perhaps no clear "Thou" at all. Perhaps even other people are merely extensions of the "I," reflections of it, modifications of it, aspects of it. Perhaps for this "I" there is no clear distinction between itself and other objects: it may find itself immersed in a world of objects, and to have lost its own subjectivity, even though it may be very conscious and even aggressively definite in saying "I."

If such an "I" one day hears about "contemplation," he will perhaps set himself to "become contemplative." That is, he will wish to admire, in himself, something called contemplation. And, in order to see it, he will reflect on his alienated self. He will make contemplative faces at himself like a child in front of a mirror. He will cultivate the contemplative look that seems appropriate to him and that he likes to see in himself. And the fact that his busy narcissism is turned within and feeds upon itself in stillness and secret love will make him believe that his experience of himself is an experience of God.

But the exterior "I," the "I" of projects, of temporal finalities, the "I" that manipulates objects in order to take possession of them, is alien from the hidden, interior "I" who has no projects and seeks to accomplish nothing, even contemplation. He seeks only to be, and to move (for he is dynamic) according to the secret laws of Being itself, and according to the promptings of a Superior Freedom (that is, of God), rather than to plan and to achieve according to his own desires . . .

. . . The inner self is precisely that self which cannot be tricked or manipulated by anyone, even by the devil. He is like a very shy wild animal that never appears at all whenever an alien presence is at hand, and comes out only when all is perfectly peaceful, in silence, when he is untroubled and alone. He cannot be lured by anyone or anything, because he responds to no lure except that of the divine freedom . . . [pp. 4–5]

. . . The inner self is not a part of our being, like a motor in a car. It is our entire substantial reality itself, on its highest and most personal and most existential level. It is like life, and it is life: it is our spiritual life when it is most alive. It is the life by which everything else in us lives and moves . . . If it is awakened, it communicates a new life to the intelligence in which it lives, so that it becomes a living awareness of itself: and this awareness is not so much something that we ourselves have as something that we are . . .

The inner self is as secret as God, and like Him, it evades every concept that tries to seize hold of it with full possession. It is a life that cannot be held and studied as an object, because it is not a "thing." It is not reached and coaxed forth from hiding by any process under the sun, including meditation. All we can do with any spiritual discipline is produce within ourselves something of the silence, the humility, the detachment, the purity of heart, and the indifference which are required if the inner self is to make some shy, unpredictable manifestation of his presence.

At the same time, however, every deeply spiritual experience, whether religious or moral, or even artistic, tends to have in it something of the presence of the interior self. Only from the inner self does any spiritual experience gain depth, reality, and a certain incommunicability. But the depth of ordinary experience only gives us a derivative sense of the inner self. It reminds us of the forgotten levels of interiority in our spiritual nature, and of our helplessness to explore them. [pp. 6–7]

Nevertheless, a certain cultural and spiritual atmosphere favors the secret and spontaneous development of the inner self. The ancient cultural tradition, both of the East and of the West, having a religious and sapiential nature, favored the interior life and indeed transmitted certain common materials in the form of archetypal symbols, liturgical rites, art, poetry, philosophy, and myth which nourished the inner self from childhood to maturity. In such a cultural setting, no one needs to be self-conscious about his interior life, and subjectivity does not run the risk of being diverted into morbidity and excess. Unfortunately, such a cultural setting no longer exists in the West, or is no longer common property. It is something that has to be laboriously recovered by an educated and enlightened minority. [Handwritten insert, p. 7]

. . . The inner self is not an *ideal* self, especially not an imaginary, perfect creature fabricated to measure up to our compulsive need for greatness, heroism, and infallibility. On the contrary, the real "I" is just simply our self and nothing more. Nothing more, nothing less. Our self as we are in the eyes of God . . . Our self in all our uniqueness, dignity, littleness, and ineffable greatness: the greatness we have received from God our Father . . . [p. 10]

. . . In Zen there seems to be no effort to get *beyond* the inner self. In Christianity the inner self is simply a stepping-stone to an awareness of God. Man is the image of God, and his inner self is a kind of mirror in which God not only sees Himself but reveals Himself to the "mirror" in which He is reflected . . . If we enter into ourselves, find our true self, and then pass "beyond" the inner "I," we sail forth into the immense darkness in which we confront the "I AM" of the Almighty. The Zen writers might perhaps contend that they were interested exclusively in what is actually "given" in their experience, and that Christianity is super-adding a theological interpretation and extrapolation on top of the experience itself. But here we come upon one of the distinctive features of Christian, Jewish, and Islamic mysticisms. For us, there is an infinite metaphysical gulf between the being of God and the being of the soul, between the "I" of the Almighty and our own inner "I." Yet, paradoxically, our inmost "I" exists in God and God dwells in it. But it is nevertheless necessary to distinguish between the experience of one's inmost being and the awareness that God has revealed Himself to us in and through our inner self. We must know that the mirror is distinct from the image reflected in it. The difference rests on theological faith . . . Our awareness of God is a supernatural participation in the light by which He reveals Himself interiorly as dwelling in our inmost self. Hence, the Christian mystical experience is not only an awareness of the inner self but also, by a supernatural intensification of faith, it is an experiential grasp of God as present within our inner self. [pp. 10–11]

. . . There is always the possibility that what an Eastern mystic describes as Self is what the Western mystic will describe as God, because we shall see presently that the mystical union between the soul and God renders them in some sense "undivided" (though metaphysically distinct) in spiritual experience. And the fact that the Eastern mystic, not conditioned by centuries of theological debate, may not be inclined to reflect on the fine points of metaphysical distinction does not necessarily mean that he has not experienced the presence of God when he speaks of knowing the Inmost Self. [p. 12]

. . . The contemplative does not cease to *know* external objects. But he ceases to be *guided* by them. He ceases to depend on them. He ceases to treat them as ultimate. He evaluates them in a new way in which they are no longer objects of desire or fear but remain neutral and, as it were, empty until such times as they, too, are filled with the light of God. [p. 15]

. . . At the end of this journey of faith and love which brings us into the depths of our own being and releases us that we may voyage beyond ourselves to God, the mystical life culminates in an experience of the presence of God that is beyond all description, and which is only possible because the soul has been completely "transformed in God" so as to become, so to speak, "one spirit" with Him . . .

. . . Since our inmost "I" is the perfect image of God, then when that "I" awakens he finds within himself the Presence of Him Whose image he is. And, by a paradox beyond all human expression, God and the soul seem to have but one single "I." They are (by divine grace) as though one single person. They breathe and live and act as one. "Neither" of the "two" is seen as object.

To anyone who has full awareness of our "exile" from God, our alienation from this inmost self, and our blind wandering in the "region of unlikeness," this claim can hardly seem believable. Yet it is nothing else but the message of Christ calling us to awake from sleep, to return from exile and find our true selves within ourselves, in that inner sanctuary which is His temple and His heaven, and (at the end of the prodigal's homecoming journey) the "Father's House." [p. 16]

. . . Though a certain introversion and detachment are necessary in order to reestablish the proper conditions for the "awakening" of what is inmost in ourselves, the spiritual "I" obviously stands in a definite relationship to the world of objects. All the more is it related to the world of other personal subjects . . .

Instead of seeing the external world in its bewildering complexity, separateness, and multiplicity; instead of seeing objects as things to be manipulated for pleasure or profit; instead of placing ourselves over against objects in a posture of desire, defiance, suspicion, greed, or fear, the inner self sees the world from a deeper and more spiritual viewpoint. In the language of Zen, it sees things "without affirmation or denial"; that is to say, from a higher vantage point, which is intuitive and concrete and which has no need to manipulate or distort reality by means of slanted concepts and judgments. It simply "sees" what it sees, and does not take refuge behind a screen of conceptual prejudices and verbalistic distortions. [p. 17]

. . . The inner self sees the other not as a limitation upon itself but as its complement, its "other self," and is even in a certain sense identified with that other, so that the two "are one." This unity in love is one of the most characteristic works of the inner self, so that paradoxically the inner "I" is not only isolated but at the same time united with others on a higher plane, which is in fact the plane of spiritual solitude. And this is one of the most characteristic features of Christian contemplative awareness. The Christian is not merely "alone with the Alone" in the Neoplatonic sense, but he is One with all his "brothers in Christ." His inner self is, in fact, inseparable from Christ and hence it is in a mysterious and unique way inseparable from all the other "I"s who live in Christ, so that they all form one "mystical Person," which is "Christ." [pp. 19–20]

. . . The inner "I" is certainly the sanctuary of our most personal and individual solitude, and yet, paradoxically, it is precisely that which is most solitary and personal in ourselves which is united with the "Thou" who confronts us. We are not capable of union with one another on the deepest level until the inner self in each one of us is sufficiently awakened to confront the inmost spirit of the other. This mutual recognition is love "in the Spirit," and is effected, indeed, by the Holy Spirit. [p. 20]

. . . The awakening of the inner self is purely the work of love, and there can be no love where there is not "another" to love. Furthermore, one does not awaken his inmost "I" merely by loving God alone, but by loving other men. [p. 21]

. . . Solitude is necessary for spiritual freedom. But once that freedom is acquired, it demands to be put to work in the service of a love in which there is no longer subjection or slavery. Mere withdrawal, without the return to freedom in action, would lead to a static and death-like inertia of the spirit in which the inner self would not awaken at all. [p. 22]

. . . All truly serious and spiritual forms of religion aspire at least implicitly to a contemplative awakening both of the individual and of the group. But those forms of religious and liturgical worship which have lost their initial impulse of fervor tend more and more to forget their contemplative purpose and to attach exclusive importance to rites and forms for their own sake, or for the sake of the effect which they are believed to exercise on the One Who is worshipped. [p. 23]

As we grow in knowledge and appreciation of Oriental religion, we will come to realize the depth and richness of its varied forms of contemplation. [p. 30]

. . . In fact, contemplation is man's highest and most essential spiritual activity. It is his most creative and dynamic affirmation of his divine sonship . . . It is a flash of the lightning of divinity piercing the darkness of nothingness and sin. Not something general and abstract, but something, on the contrary, as concrete, particular, and "existential" as it can possibly be. It is the confrontation of man with his God, of the son with his Father. It is the awakening of Christ within us, the establishment of the Kingdom of God in our souls, the triumph of the Truth of Divine Freedom in the inmost "I" in which the Father becomes one with the Son in the Spirit who is given to the believer. [p. 33]

The story of Adam's fall from Paradise says, in symbolic terms, that man was created as a contemplative. The fall from Paradise was a fall from unity . . . Man fell from the unity of contemplative vision into the multiplicity, complication, and distraction of an active worldly existence . . . In such a condition, man's mind is enslaved by an inexorable concern with all that is exterior, transient, illusory, and trivial . . . He is utterly exiled from God and from his own true self . . .

He is tempted to seek God and happiness outside himself. So his quest for happiness becomes, in fact, a flight from God and from himself: a flight that takes him further and further away from reality.

But man must return to paradise. He must recover himself, salvage his dignity, recollect his lost wits, return to his true identity. There is only one way in which this could be done, says the Gospel of Christ. God Himself must come, like the woman in the parable seeking the lost groat. God Himself must become Man in order that, in the God-Man, man might be able to lose himself as man and find himself as God. God Himself must die on the cross, leaving man a pattern and a proof of His infinite love. And man, communing with God in the death and resurrection of Christ, must die the spiritual death in which his exterior self is destroyed and his inner self rises from death by faith and lives again "unto God."

The Christian life is a return to the Father, the Source,

the Ground of all existence, through the Son, the Splendor and the Image of the Father, in the Holy Spirit, the Love of the Father and the Son. And this return is only possible by detachment and "death" in the exterior self, so that the inner self, purified and renewed, can fulfill its function as image of the Divine Trinity. [pp. 34–35]

. . . Of course, Christ has taken possession of our souls and bodies, and we are already divinized, in the roots of our being, by baptism. But this divine life remains hidden and dormant within us unless it is more fully developed by a life of asceticism and charity and, on a higher level, of contemplation. We not only passively receive in us the grace of Christ, but we actively renew in our own life the self-emptying and self-transformation by which God became man. Just as the Word "emptied Himself" of His divine and transcendent nobility in order to "descend" to the level of man, so we must empty ourselves of what is human in the ignoble sense of the word, which really means less than human, in order that we may become God. This does not mean the sacrifice or destruction of anything that really belongs to our human nature as it was assumed by Christ, but it means the complete, radical cutting off of everything in us that was *not* assumed by Him because it was not capable of being divinized. And what is this? It is everything that is focused on our exterior and self-centered passion, as self-assertion, greed, lust; as the desire for the survival and perpetuation of our illusory and superficial self, to the detriment of our interior and true self. [pp. 39–40]

In active contemplation, there is a deliberate and sustained effort to detect the will of God in events and to bring one's whole self into harmony with that will . . . Along with this, there is a deep concern with the symbolic and ritual enactment of those sacred mysteries which represent the divine actions by which the redemption and sanctification of the world is effected. In other words, active contemplation rests on a deep ground of liturgical, historical, and cultural tradition—but a living tradition, not dead convention. And a tradition still in dynamic movement and growth. The contemplative mind is, in fact, not normally ultraconservative; but neither is it necessarily radical. It transcends both these extremes in order to remain in living contact with that which is genuinely true in any traditional movement. Hence, the contemplative mind today will not normally be associated too firmly or too definitively with any "movement," whether political, religious, liturgical, artistic, philosophical, or what have you. The contemplative stays clear of movements, not because they confuse him, but simply because he does not need them and can go further by himself than he can in their formalized and often fanatical ranks.

Nevertheless, active contemplation should be to a great extent in contact with the *logos* of its age. Which means in simple fact that the contemplative today might be expected to have an intuitive grasp of and even sympathy for what is most genuine in the characteristic movements of our time —Marxism, existentialism, psychoanalysis, eirenism. [pp. 55–56]

In active contemplation, a man becomes able to live within himself. He learns to be at home with his own thoughts. He becomes to a greater and greater degree independent of exterior supports. His mind is pacified not by passive dependence on things outside himself—diversions, entertainments, conversations, business—but by its own constructive activity. That is to say that he derives inner satisfaction from spiritual creativeness: thinking his own thoughts, reaching his own conclusions, looking at his own life and directing it in accordance with his own inner truth, discovered in meditation and under the eyes of God. [p. 57]

Reading becomes contemplative when, instead of reasoning, we abandon the sequence of the author's thought in order not only to follow our own thoughts (meditation) but simply *to rise above thought and penetrate into the mystery of truth which is experienced intuitively as present and actual.* We meditate with our mind, which is "part of" our being. But we contemplate with our whole being and not just with one of its parts. [p. 57]

[The Greek Fathers draw a distinction] between natural contemplation *(theoria physike)* and theology *(theologia),* or the contemplation of God.
Theoria physike is the intuition of divine things in and through the reflection of God in nature and in the symbols of revelation . . .
Theoria physike is contemplation of the divine *in nature,* not contemplation of the divine by our natural powers.
Theologia, or pure contemplation ("mystical theology," in the language of Pseudo-Denis), is a direct quasi-experiential contact with God beyond all thought; that is to say, without the medium of concepts. This excludes not only concepts tinged with passion, or sentimentality, or imagination, but even the simplest intellectual intuitions that require some sort of medium between God and the spirit. Theology in this sense is a direct contact with God. [pp. 66–67]

. . . The inner self of the mystic, elevated and transformed in Christ, united to the Father in the Son, through the Holy Spirit, now knows God not so much through the medium of an objective image as through its own divinized subjectivity . . . Thoughts, natural light, and spiritual images are, so to speak, veils or coverings that impede the direct, naked sensitivity by which the spirit touches the Divine Being. When the veils are removed, then one can touch, or rather be touched by, God, in the mystical darkness. Intuition reaches Him by one final leap beyond itself, an ecstasy in which it sacrifices itself and yields itself to His transcendent presence. In this last ecstatic act of "unknowing," the gap between our spirit as subject and God as object is finally closed, and in the embrace of mystical love we know that we and He are one. This is infused or mystical contemplation in the purest sense of the term. [pp. 68–69]

. . . When we begin to be frequently absorbed in the passivity of pre-experiential contemplation . . . we feel that we are losing our ability to meditate and pray. Not only that, but we believe, and even have evidence for the fact, that we are not as virtuous as we had thought. (This realization is of course one of the most valuable and enviable effects of infused prayer!) We begin to see the nonentity and triviality of our exterior self: and since we are still completely identified with that exterior self, this means that, to all intents and purposes, we begin to experience ourselves as evil, ungodly, hypocritical, and utterly contemptible beings. We *should* experience this. For as long as we live in our exterior consciousness alone and identify ourselves completely with the superficial and transient side of our existence, then we are completely immersed in unreality. And to cling with passion to a state of unreality is the root of all sin: technically known as pride. It is the affirmation of our nonbeing as the ultimate reality for which we live, as against the being and truth of God. Hence, we must become detached from the unreality that is in us in order to be united to the reality that lies deeper within and is our true self—our inmost self-in-God. [pp. 86–87]

Both the existentialist and the contemplative are united by the depth and sincerity of their "concern." Both reject any easy or convenient substitute for ultimate reality. Both face the insecurity and darkness of spiritual risk. And here, of course, we face the need to distinguish between the religious and irreligious existentialist. The fact is that though Sartre, popularly regarded as "the" existentialist, is also an atheist, more existential thinkers are religious than otherwise. Kierkegaard, who is regarded as the father of them all, was one of the great religious geniuses of an irreligious century. Men like Gabriel Marcel (a Catholic) and Nicholas Berdyaev (a Russian Orthodox) have entered fully into his heritage. Jacques Maritain, who has written a very understanding Thomist critique of existentialism, is also a Christian contemplative whose contemplation has attuned him to the subjective sorrow and sincerity of existentialism while protecting him from its nihilistic dangers. It is clear that if a dialogue is to take place between Christians and the subjectivists of our time, a contemplative is the one to speak for Christianity. A dogmatist, firmly entrenched in scholastic categories, has no way of making himself understood. If he is to enter a fruitful dialogue with some opposite number, he had better look to the camp of the Marxists. There, too, he will find dogma and "true believers." Whether or not he will be able to make contact with them is another matter, but in any case it should be clear that the contemplative and the Marxist have no common ground. They do not think in the same way or even see the same things at all. To be a Marxist, one would have to repress all the inner, personal "concern" with spiritual fulfillment and lose oneself in the collective mystery of the revolution. Contemplation could only interest a Marxist if it caught him on the rebound after a fall from dialectical grace, and at a moment when his interior starvation demanded, by accident, to be recognized. But a writer like Boris Pasternak, himself never a Marxist, bears witness to the intense hunger for a spiritual experience of reality which has remained alive in the arid desert of Russian materialism since 1917. Not that Pasternak is a contemplative in the full sense of the word: but his poetry and poetic prose are filled with symbolic intuitions on the order of *theoria physike,* and his view of life is in a broad sense not only Christian but mystical. This, of course, marks him out as a complete heretic in Russia, where "mysticism" is the ultimate term of contempt.

However, there is in Marxism enough of false mysticism and religiosity to seduce anyone who hungers after some substitute for spiritual religion. There is no question that the demand for "faith" and for self-sacrifice which is made by Marxism is a much more solid and human reality than the irresponsible pseudo-Christianity that still flourishes in certain societies devoted entirely to secular values. There is some spiritual danger in Marxism and in the pseudo-contemplation which its world view implies. This danger lies in a crypto-religious appeal it offers to those who have no stomach left for the empty forms of popular religion in which the concept "god" has died of exhaustion. [pp. 99–100]

. . . Once spiritual experience becomes objectified, it turns into an idol. It becomes a "thing," a "reality" which we serve. We were not created for the service of any "thing," but for the service of God alone, who is not and cannot be a "thing." To serve Him who is no "object" is freedom. To live for spiritual experience is slavery, and such slavery makes the contemplative life just as secular (though in a more subtle way) as the service of any other "thing," no matter how base: money, pleasure, success. Indeed, the ruin of many potential contemplatives has been this avidity for spiritual success. That is why at the very beginning of this essay I stressed the danger of looking for "happiness" as a goal in the life of contemplation. It is all the more dangerous because the satisfaction we derive from spiritual things is pure and perfect. And all the harder to bring under objective criticism. [pp. 100–1]

The true contemplative is a lover of sobriety and obscurity. He prefers all that is quiet, humble, unassuming. He has no taste for spiritual excitements. They easily weary him. His inclination is to that which seems to be nothing, which tells him little or nothing, which promises him nothing. Only one who can remain at peace in emptiness, without projects or vanities, without speeches to justify his own apparent uselessness, can be safe from the fatal appeal of those spiritual impulses that move him to assert himself and "be something" in the eyes of other men. But the contemplative is, of all religious men, the one most likely to realize that he is not a saint and least anxious to appear one in the eyes of others. He is, in fact, delivered from subjection to appearances, and cares very little about them. At the same time, since he has neither the inclination nor the need to be a rebel, he does not have to advertise his contempt for appearances. He simply neglects them. They no longer interest him . . . [p. 103]

. . . The contemplative life is one of intense inner conflict. The peace which it brings is a peace that follows war and exists often enough in the midst of war. Anyone who is already divided against himself and at war with himself had better get himself together before he sets out to conquer the realm of ascetic meditation and contemplative prayer. Otherwise, the divisions already present in him will tear him apart in short order.

Excursions into the recollected darkness of contemplation are tempting to anyone with a schizoid character, because it is easy to mistake schizoid withdrawal for contemplative recollection. And a few formulas of contemplative jargon may offer themselves as fatally convenient opportunities for rationalization by one who is merely escaping, within himself, from external reality.

Contemplation does not back away from reality, or evade it. It sees through superficial being, and goes beyond it. This implies a full acceptance of things as they are, and a sane evaluation of them. The "darkness" of the contemplative night is not a rejection of created things. On the contrary, the contemplative in some way "finds" and discovers things as they really are, and enjoys them in a higher way, when he rises above contacts with them that are merely sensual and superficial . . . The neurotic, on the other hand, cannot accept reality as it is. He withdraws into himself and if he sees things at all sees only that aspect of them which he can bear to see, and no other. Or at least he tries to.

Now, it is easy to understand that an unwise and Manichaean type of asceticism can give a person a pathological attitude toward reality. In such case, there is great danger of his becoming a pseudo-mystic who flees into his own inner darkness and tries to wall himself up inside his own silence. There he seeks to enjoy the false sweetness of a narcissistic seclusion, and does indeed enjoy it for a while, until he learns too late that he has poisoned himself with the fruit of a tree that is forbidden . . .

. . . The neurotic cannot help but self-consciously exploit his opportunities for spiritual "experience." He is compelled to do this, to allay his anxiety, and to justify his withdrawal from reality as a religious act. In actual fact, his contemplation is a lie, an act of idolatry, and forms part of his private religion. For such men as this, the solitude and freedom of the contemplative life lead only to ruin. They are not capable of solitude because they are not strong enough to love. [pp. 104–6]

We have returned again and again to a few simple thoughts in the preceding pages: contemplative experience is something very real but elusive and hard to define. It takes place in the depths of the subject's own spiritual being, and yet it is an "experience" of the transcendent, personal presence of God. This experience has to be carefully qualified, because its paradoxical character makes it an experiential awareness of what cannot be experienced on earth. It is knowledge of Him Who is beyond all knowledge. Hence, it knows Him as unknown. It knows by "unknowing."

This "dark knowledge," this "apophatic" grasp of Him Who is, cannot be explained in a satisfactory way to anyone who has not come to experience something of the sort in his own inner life. Yet those who have felt these things easily recognize the experience in another. And the strange thing is that the phenomenon is constant. It recurs from age to age, in all kinds of places, in all kinds of societies. And its recurrence is sufficiently easy to verify empirically, as was done by William James . . .

. . . Everywhere we find at least a natural striving for interior unity and intuitive communion with the Absolute. And everywhere we find expressions of some kind of spiritual experience, often natural, sometimes supernatural. Supernatural mystical experience is at least theoretically possible anywhere under the sun, to any man of good conscience who sincerely seeks the truth and responds to the inspirations of divine grace. [pp. 109–10]

. . . There may be much desolation and suffering in the spirit of the contemplative, but there is always more joy than sorrow, more security than doubt, more peace than desolation. The contemplative is one who has found what every man seeks in one way or other. [p. 110]

. . . The great obstacle to contemplation is rigidity and prejudice. He who thinks he knows what it is beforehand prevents himself from finding out the true nature of contemplation, since he is not able to "change his mind" and accept something completely new. He who thinks that contemplation is lofty and spectacular cannot receive the intuition of a supreme and transcendent Reality which is at the same time immanent in his own ordinary self. [p. 111]

The first step toward spiritual liberation is not so much the awareness of what lies at the end of the road—the experience of God—as a clear view of the great obstacle that blocks its very beginning. That obstacle is called sin. A great reality, a very great mystery . . .

. . . [The sense of sin] is not merely a sense of guilt referred to the authority of God. It is a sense of evil in myself. Not because I have violated a law outside myself, but because I have violated the inmost laws of my own being, which are, at the same time, the laws of God Who dwells within me. The sense of sin is the sense of having been deeply and deliberately false to my inmost reality, my likeness to God . . . To have a sense of sin is to realize myself to be not only morally but spiritually dead. Moral death would savor rather of guilt—I have been "killed" by the violation of a law. But spiritual death is the sense of

having separated myself from truth by complete inner falsity, from love by selfishness, from reality by trying to assert
as real a will to nothingness. The sense of sin is then something ontological and immediate which does not spring
from reflection on my actions and comparison with a moral
code. It springs directly from the evil that is present in me:
it tells me not merely that I have done wrong but that I *am*
wrong, through and through. That I am a false being. That
I have destroyed myself. [pp. 112–13]

Hence, part of the mission of the contemplative is to
keep alive in the world the sense of sin. In this, he is the
descendant of the Old Testament prophets, for that too
was their mission. They had to confront the Jewish people
at every moment with the reality of sin, which cut them off
from God, as distinct from ritual guilt, which could be set
right with legal ceremonies. This was no pleasant vocation, because it was something more difficult and mysterious than the mere preaching of morality. Jeremias had
not only to teach justice and mercy but also to persuade
the people to accept the concrete will of God for them.
[p. 114]

The contemplative is one who is, like the servant of Yah-
weh, "acquainted with infirmity," not only with his own sin
but with the sin of the whole world, which he takes upon
himself because he is a man among men, and cannot dissociate himself from the works of other men. The contemplative life in our time is therefore necessarily modified by the
sins of our age. They bring down upon us a cloud of darkness far more terrible than the innocent night of unknowing. It is the dark night of the soul which has descended on
the whole world. Contemplation, in the age of Auschwitz
and Dachau, Solovky and Karaganda, is something darker

and more fearsome than contemplation in the age of the Church Fathers. [pp. 114–15]

The monastic life as it exists today often presupposes too much in the young postulant who seeks admission. It presupposes that he knows his own mind, that he is capable of making a mature decision, that he has grown up, that he has received a liberal education. It is often discovered too late that such things cannot be taken for granted. Before the average youth of today is ready for monastic life, his senses, feelings, and imagination need to be re-formed and educated along normal natural lines. Americans under twenty-one who present themselves at the monastery gate are not usually full-blooded mature men with strong passions that need to be disciplined and mortified, but confused kids with a complex bundle of vague emotional fears and desires going in all directions at once. They are a pitiful mixture of pseudo-sophistication and utter vacuity. They are not only not ready for the contemplative life, but they are not ready for any kind of life. [pp. 119–20]

. . . There is nothing in any monastic rule that foresees the arrival in a monastery of a television addict . . . [p. 120]

In the pre-industrial ages and in primitive societies that still exist, man is naturally prepared and disposed for contemplation. In such a world we find men who, though perhaps not all literate, possess traditional artistic and technical skills and are in a broad sense "artists" and "spiritual men." They are formed by their tradition and their culture. Even though such men may not be able to read and write, they are not necessarily "ignorant." On the contrary, they possess a certain very important and vital kind of knowledge, and *all of it* is integrated into their lives. They have a wholeness and a humanity, and therefore a poise, a simplicity, and a confidence which have vanished from a world in which men are alienated, enslaved to processes and machines. Pre-industrial man is therefore all ready to become a contemplative. Indeed, it can be said that, in the past, whole societies were oriented quite naturally to a spiritual and even contemplative life. [pp. 121–122]

... It seems right to say that one who wants a contemplative life today, whether he is in a monastery or in the world, must do two things. First, he must as far as possible reduce the conflict and frustration in his life by cutting down his contact with the "world" and his secular subjections. This means reducing his needs for pleasure, comfort, recreation, prestige, and success, and embracing a life of true spiritual poverty and detachment. Second, he must learn to put up with the inevitable conflicts that remain—the noise, the agitation, the crowding, the lack of time, and above all the constant contact with a purely secular mentality which is all around us everywhere and at all times, even to some extent in monasteries. [p. 131]

Sunday is a day of contemplation not because it is a day without work, a day when the shops and banks and offices are closed. But because it is sacred to the mystery of the Resurrection. Sunday is the "Lord's Day," not in the sense that, on one day out of the week, one must stop and think of Him, but because it breaks into the ceaseless "secular" round of time with a burst of light out of a sacred eternity. We must stop working and rushing about on Sunday, not only in order to rest up and start over again on Monday, but in order to collect our wits and realize the relative meaninglessness of the secular business which fills the other six days of the week, and taste the satisfaction of a peace which surpasses understanding and which is given us by Christ. Sunday reminds us of the peace that should filter through the whole week when our week is properly oriented. Sunday is a contemplative day not just because Church Law demands that every Christian assist at Mass but because everyone, Christian or not, who celebrates the day spiritually and accepts it at its face value opens his heart to the light of Christ, the light of the Resurrection. In so doing, he grows in love, in faith, and is able to "see" a little more of the mystery of Christ. He certainly may have no clear idea of what is happening, but the grace of God produces its effects in his heart. Sunday, then, is a day of grace, a day of light, in which light is given. Simple fidelity to this obvious duty, realization of this gift of God, will certainly help the harassed layman to take his first steps on the path to a kind of contemplation. [pp. 133–34]

. . . Active virtue and good works play a large part in the "contemplative" life that is led in the world, and the uncloistered man of prayer is most likely to be what we have called a "masked contemplative." [p. 134]

The discipline of the contemplative in the world is, first of all, the discipline of fidelity to his duty of state—to his obligations as head of a family, as a member of a profession, as a citizen . . . [p. 134]

. . . For the married Christian, his married life is essentially bound up with his contemplation. This is inevitable. It is by his marriage that he is situated in the mystery of Christ. It is by his marriage that he bears witness to Christ's love for the world, and in his marriage that he experiences that love. His marriage is a sacramental center from which grace radiates out into every department of his life, and consequently it is his marriage that will enable his work, his leisure, his sacrifices, and even his distractions to become in some degree contemplative. For by his marriage all these things are ordered to Christ and centered in Christ. [p. 135]

. . . A contemplative is not just a man who stays apart from other men and meditates while they struggle to make their living. He is not just a man who forgets about the world, with its political or cultural upheavals, and sits absorbed in prayer while bombers swarm in the air over his monastery. Most of the trouble with the contemplative life today comes from this purely negative approach.

The contemplative life is primarily a life of *unity*. A contemplative is one who has transcended divisions to reach a unity beyond division. It is true that he must begin by separating himself from the ordinary activities of men, to some extent. He must recollect himself, turn within, in order to find the inner center of spiritual activity which remains inaccessible as long as he is immersed in the exterior business of life. But, once he has found this center, it is very important that he realize what comes next.

Very many frustrated contemplatives are people who have managed to break away from exterior distractions and find their way to the spiritual center of their being. They have become momentarily aware of God and of the possibilities of the contemplative life. But they have imagined that the way to live it was to sit still, curled up upon themselves, coddling the inner experience which they had discovered. This is a fatal misconception. First of all, it isolates the contemplative within himself, and cuts him off from all other realities. But in this way he becomes engrossed and absorbed in himself. His introversion leads to a kind of torpid imprisonment in himself, and this, of course, is the ruin of all true contemplation.

Contemplation must not be confused with abstraction. A contemplative life is not to be lived by permanent withdrawal within one's own mind. The diminished and limited existence of a small, isolated, specialized group is not enough for "contemplation." The true contemplative is not less interested than others in normal life, not less concerned with what goes on in the world, but *more* interested, more concerned. The fact that he is a contemplative makes him capable of a greater interest and of a deeper concern. Since he is detached, since he has received the gift of a pure heart, he is not limited to narrow and provincial views. He is not easily involved in the superficial confusion which most men take for reality. And for that reason he can see more clearly and enter more directly into the pure actuality of human life. The thing that distinguishes him from other men, and gives him a distinct advantage over them, is that he has a much more spiritual grasp of what is "real" and what is "actual."

This does not mean that the contemplative mind has a deeper practical insight into political or economic affairs. Nor that the contemplative can beat the mathematician or engineer at their own games. In all that seems most practical and urgent to other men, the contemplative may distinguish himself perhaps only by ineptitude and near-folly. But he still has the inestimable gift of appreciating, at their real worth, values that are permanent, authentically deep, human, truly spiritual, and even divine.

This means that the contemplative is not simply a specialist in a certain esoteric spiritual field. If he is no more than this, he has failed in his vocation. No, his mission is to be a complete and whole man, with an instinctive and generous need to further the same wholeness in others, and in all mankind. He arrives at this, however, not by superior gifts and special talents, but by the simplicity and poverty which are essential to his state because they alone keep him traveling in the way that is spiritual, divine, and beyond understanding.

He is one who is best attuned to the logos of man's present situation, immersed in its mystery, acquainted with its deepest suffering, and sensitive to its most viable hopes. He is the one who is in harmony with the *Tao*. Hence, he cannot help but look at the world attentively and with much more understanding than the politician who thinks himself in command. The contemplative knows who is in command, and knows whom to obey, though he does not always understand the commands any more than others do. [pp. 142–44]

. . . The "reality" through which the contemplative "penetrates" in order to reach a contact with what is "ultimate" in it is actually his own being, his own life. The contemplative is not one who directs a magic spiritual intuition upon other objects but one who, being perfectly unified in himself, and recollected in the center of his own humility, enters into contact with reality by an immediacy that forgets the division between subject and object. In a certain sense, by losing himself, and by forgetting himself as an object of reflection, he finds himself and all other reality together. This "finding" is beyond concepts and beyond practical projects. [pp. 147–48]

The contemplative life is, then, a matter of the greatest importance for modern man, and is important to him in all that is most valuable to his ideal. Today more than ever, man in chains is seeking emancipation and liberty. His tragedy is that he seeks it by means that bring him into ever greater enslavement. But freedom is a spiritual thing. It is a sacred and religious reality. Its roots are not in man but in God. For man's freedom, which makes him the image of

God, is a participation in the freedom of God. Man is free insofar as he is like God. His struggle for freedom means, then, a struggle to renounce a false, illusory autonomy, in order to become free beyond and above himself. In other words, for man to be free he must be delivered *from himself:* for the tyranny of man over man is but the external expression of each man's enslavement to his own desires. For he who is the slave of his own desires necessarily exploits others, in order to pay tribute to the tyrant within himself.

Before there can be any external freedom, man must learn to find the way to freedom within himself. For only then can he afford to relax his grip on others, and let them get away from him, because then he does not need their dependence. It is the contemplative who keeps this liberty alive in the world, and who shows others, obscurely, and without realizing it, what real freedom means.

That was why St. Gregory of Nyssa said that the contemplative, who had restored in his own soul the image of God, was the truly free man: for he alone could walk with God, as Adam had walked with Him in Paradise. He alone could stand and speak freely to God His Father, with complete confidence. He alone could worthily bear his dignity as son of God and king of God's creation . . . [pp. 149–150]

VI

New Seeds of Contemplation

Seeds of Contemplation, published in 1949, was reprinted at least ten times. Beginning with the seventh printing, published December 19, 1949, the book was issued in a revised edition.* This revision, though not substantive with regard to content, is different in outlook from the original edition. In 1962 a second revision was published which not only picked up and amplified the new outlook evident in the first revision but was sufficiently altered and enlarged in content to justify Merton's statement in the preface that "it is in many ways a completely new book," and to warrant the use of the adjective "New" in the title of this final revision.†

*On July 9, 1949, Merton wrote to Jacques Maritain: "I am revising *Seeds of Contemplation,* in which many statements are hasty and do not express my true meaning" (Files of the Merton Studies Center, Louisville, Ky.).

†Donald Grayston has clarified the differences among the three editions in this way: "*Seeds* and *Seeds Revised* share a common framework, but differ in tone; *Seeds Revised* and *New Seeds* share a common tone but differ in framework; . . . *Seeds* and *New Seeds* differ in both tone and framework." In Donald Grayston, "The Making of a Spiritual Classic: Thomas Merton's *Seeds of Contemplation* and *New Seeds of Contemplation,* " *Sciences Religieuses/Studies in Religion,* 3 (1973–74), p. 339.

Seeds of Contemplation proved to be a very popular book, as the number of printings testify; nor was its popularity confined to English-speaking readers: it has been translated into thirteen languages.* *New Seeds of Contemplation,* which is the only edition remaining in print, has continued to be a favorite among longtime Merton readers, as also among those who have just recently "discovered" Merton.† *New Seeds* has had five foreign-language translations.

The purpose of this chapter is to explore the new insights into the contemplative experience that a reading of *New Seeds* will offer to one who has already read *Seeds of Contemplation.* What is the difference in outlook and in content that one finds in the third edition of this "spiritual classic"?‡ One way of answering this question is to consider what Merton himself has to say about the three different editions. Each of the three versions has an Author's Note. In addition, each of the two later versions has a preface in which Merton introduces the new version to his readers.

The Author's Note is identical in the first and second editions. There is, however, an interesting addition and an equally interesting omission in the Author's Note of *New Seeds.* The addition is a footnote appended to the statement "These are the kinds of thoughts that might have occurred to any Cistercian monk." In the footnote Merton writes, not without a touch of humor, that not all his confreres saw

---

*Chinese, Danish, French, German, Italian, Japanese, Korean, Dutch, Polish, Portuguese, Spanish, Swedish, Vietnamese; *New Seeds* has been translated into French, German, Italian, Portuguese, and Spanish. See Robert E. Daggy, *Thomas Merton's Major Writings: A Bibliographic Checklist* (Merton Studies Center, Louisville, Ky.).

†The writer has taught Merton seminars to college students and can testify to the favorite-book status of *New Seeds* among these students.

‡Donald Grayston and Aldhelm Cameron-Brown have both used the term "spiritual classic" to describe the third edition of *Seeds.* No doubt they echo the thought of many others.

his work as representative of authentic Cistercian tradition: "In the twelve years since this was written and published, not a few Cistercians have vehemently denied that these thoughts were either characteristic or worthy of a normal Cistercian, which is perhaps quite true."

The omission in the Author's Note of *New Seeds* is even more significant. In the two earlier versions, Merton had expressed the hope that his book did not "contain a line that is new to Catholic tradition or a single word that would perplex an orthodox theologian." In *New Seeds,* the text is revised to read: "We sincerely hope that it does not contain a line that is new to Christian tradition." The substitution of the word "Christian" for "Catholic" indicates that Merton had a wider readership in mind for *New Seeds.* The fact that he is no longer worried that his writing might "perplex an orthodox theologian" suggests a broadening of his theological perspective and a movement toward a theology that would be less rigid and more pluralistic than the theological framework he had felt obliged to write in during his earlier days in the monastery. Merton is serving notice that a new type of writing could be expected from him in the future: something simpler, less abstract, and more existential. David had become uncomfortable in Saul's armor!

The movement away from a strict dogmatic framework had already been foreshadowed in the preface to the revised edition. Merton warns his readers not to search his book for precise theological statements. "The author is talking about spiritual things from the point of view of experience rather than in the concise terms of dogmatic theology." This is not only a warning but a promise: a promise of the experiential direction that Merton's writings will take in the future. It must be said that his next work on the spiritual life, *The Ascent to Truth,* did not fulfill this promise: for it is cast largely in a dogmatic framework. (But, as was already pointed out, Merton was less than satisfied with this book.)* The promise does find fulfillment in *The Inner Experience*, which, except for the older material incorporated into it, has a perspective that is definitely experiential and existential. Indeed, *The Inner Experience* may be seen as a kind of watershed between the theological ratiocinations of *What Is Contemplation* and *The Ascent to Truth* and the obvious emphasis on experience that characterizes *New Seeds, Zen and the Birds of Appetite,* the essays in *Contemplation in a World of Action, The Climate of Monastic Prayer,* as well as other works not so immediately related to the topic of contemplation. The promise made in the preface to the revised edition of *Seeds* finds ample fulfillment in Merton's later writings.

The preface of *New Seeds,* written twelve years later, reaffirms Merton's commitment to write about spiritual things in the light of experience. But between the writing of these two prefaces an important change had taken place in Merton's understanding of "experience." By 1962, "experience" had taken on a broader and deeper meaning for him. The "experience" of which he spoke in the preface to the revised edition of *Seeds* was the limited experience of a young monk who just eight years earlier had fled the world and exchanged its gregariousness for the isolation of a Trappist monastery and who, moreover, reveled in that isolation, dreaming of an even deeper withdrawal from the world as he wrestled with the "temptation" of becoming a Carthusian. There is a touch of truth in the caricature Merton draws of himself as "the man who spurned New York, spat on Chicago and tromped on Louisville, heading for the woods with Thoreau in one pocket, John of the Cross in another and holding the Bible open at the Apocalypse."

---

*Besides, he was already working on the manuscript that was to become *The Ascent to Truth* when he wrote this preface to the revised edition of *Seeds.*

The twelve years following the publication of *Seeds* were important years of growth for Merton. His flight from the world came to be tempered by a compassion for people and a growing sense that if his contemplation was to be authentic, he must "learn to share with others their joys, their sufferings, their ideas, their needs, their desires." In *Seeds,* Merton speaks of unity with others, but it is a unity discovered in prayer, rather than a grasp of solidarity with other men that is brought to prayer, so that unity can be experienced at a deeper level. In *New Seeds,* the intuition of unity is more concrete and existential. In the first two versions of *Seeds,* the locus of contemplation is "a citadel"; in *New Seeds,* it is "a wide impregnable country." As Donald Grayston has pointed out: "Both [terms] are images of security in the life of the spirit; but the first suggests enclosure, the second openness and freedom. In the citadel dwells one inhabitant; in the wide country there is room for an infinite number."

Contemplation demands solitude—a proper withdrawal from the world—and Merton was always faithful to that demand. But solitude does not mean isolation from concern for people. Indeed, such concern is the very condition for fruitful contemplation. "Contemplation is out of the question for anyone who does not try to cultivate compassion for other men."

During the twelve years that preceded the writing of *New Seeds,* Merton's contacts with others within the monastery broadened, as he was given the responsibility of directing the scholastics and later the novices. His contacts with people outside the monastery grew also, as his correspondence (including much fan mail generated by his writings) expanded and as increasing numbers of people arrived at the monastery gate to seek his counsel and to share their experiences with him. He became better informed on events and movements going on in the world, as friends sent him clippings, articles, and books, soliciting his interest and the power of his pen to shed the light of Christian truth on the social issues of the day. It is interesting—even somewhat amusing—to compare in the three editions of *Seeds* the changing "counsel" he gives his readers about the reading of newspapers:

(First edition) "Do not read their newspapers, if you can help it."

(Second edition) "Do not read their newspapers, unless you are really obliged to keep track of what is going on."

(New Seeds) "Do not read their advertisements." As he moved from the "citadel" to the "wide impregnable country,". new realms of experience opened up for him that he could carry back with him to his solitude—a solitude in which he could probe not only the depths of his own heart but, increasingly, the deepest realities of the heart of the world.

New Seeds was written in solitude, but it was a solitude that had been enriched by contact with the solitude and loneliness of many other people. Merton expressed it well in the preface to *New Seeds:*

> More than twelve years has passed between the first and second redactions of this text. When the book was first written, the author had no experience in confronting the needs and problems of other men. The book was written in a kind of isolation, in which the author was alone with his own experience of the contemplative life . . . The second writing has been no less solitary than the first: but the author's solitude has been modified by contact with other solitudes; with the loneliness, the simplicity, the perplexity of novices and scholastics of his monastic community; with the loneliness of people outside any monastery; with the loneliness of people outside the Church.

In all three versions of *Seeds,* Merton is writing about what he had experienced; but by the time he came to write *New Seeds,* "experience" had taken on new and richer meanings. Its horizons had been vastly broadened. Though he remained ever the man of solitude, the author of *New Seeds* was able to take the world, with its agonies and ecstasies, into the heart of his solitude. That is why *New Seeds,* rather than either of its predecessors, is the "spiritual classic."

Anyone who attempts to articulate the contemplative experience must choose some kind of conceptual context in which to place what he has to say about that experience. Only then can he hope to make his experience in some way intelligible to others.

In his early writings on contemplation, notably in *The Ascent to Truth,* Merton chose as his context the traditional Western approach to mystical writing represented, at its best, by St. Thomas Aquinas and St. John of the Cross. This approach stresses the activities of the various faculties of the soul—memory, imagination, intellect, and will—involved in the activity of prayer. It sharply distinguishes the supernatural activities of these faculties—elevated by the infused virtues and the gifts of the Holy Spirit—from their natural mode of operation. Such an approach assumes the body-soul dichotomy and speaks of prayer as the activity of the soul. It is an approach that tends to be abstract, highly analytical, and often unduly complex. Abounding in precise definitions, subtle distinctions, and minute explanations, it is inclined to be overly cerebral and, in the hands of writers less gifted than Thomas Aquinas and John of the Cross, to take the life and exhilaration out of the description of prayer.

As we have already seen, Merton had served notice in the preface to the revised edition of *Seeds* (December 1949) that he was abandoning this approach in writing about contemplation. What he did not mention in that preface

was that at that very time he was already one year into the
final writing of a book in this scholastic tradition.* Whatever is to be thought about Merton's inconsistency in saying in December 1949 that he would no longer write about
spiritual things "in the concise terms of dogmatic theology," when he was in the midst of writing a book that did
just that, it is quite clear that in 1962, when he came to
publish *New Seeds,* Merton had without doubt gotten the
scholastic approach out of his system.

The conceptual context of *New Seeds* is worlds apart from
the scholastic setting out of which *The Ascent to Truth*
emerged. It is a context that cannot be clearly identified. It
is, one might venture to say, a mixed context, including
elements of existentialism, Christian personalism, and Zen.
There are existential insights. Thus, for example, he writes:
"For the contemplative there is no *cogito* ('I think') and no
ergo ('therefore'), but only SUM, I am." He speaks also of
"the tragic anguish of doubt mercilessly examining the
spurious 'faith' of everyday life"—surely an existentialist
theme. There are also insights of Christian personalism
which Merton undoubtedly adopted from his friend of
many years, Jacques Maritain. The note of personalism is
introduced early in the text.

> We must remember that this superficial "I" is not our real
> self. It is our "individuality" and our "empirical self," but it
> is not truly the hidden and mysterious person in whom we
> subsist before the eyes of God.

Indeed, Christian contemplation, he writes, is "supremely
personalistic."

There is also, one is tempted to say especially, in the
context of *New Seeds,* the influence and flavor of Zen. From

---

*This book, begun in December 1948 as *The Cloud and the Fire,* was finally completed in 1951 as *The Ascent to Truth.* In February 1949 he had spoken of it as a book
on the *theology* of contemplation.

the very beginning, the book abounds in expressions, intuitions, insights, and nuances that suggest the presence of Zen. Contemplation, like Zen, cannot be taught. "It is impossible for one man to teach another 'how to become a contemplative.' One might as well write a book: 'how to be an angel.' " Moreover, contemplation, again like Zen, "cannot be clearly explained." It cannot be captured in definitions or distinctions. "It can only be hinted at, suggested, pointed to (a typical Zen term), symbolized." The more one tries to analyze it, "the more he empties it of its real content, for it is beyond the reach of verbalization and rationalization." It is, moreover, beyond the duality of knowing or unknowing. There is no adequate psychology of contemplation, for contemplation is not to be found in the superficial consciousness which can be reached by reflection.

> This reflection and this consciousness are precisely part of that external self which "dies" and is cast aside like a soiled garment in the genuine awakening of the contemplative.

For contemplation is nothing less than "life itself, fully awake, fully alive, fully aware that it is alive."

To describe an experience as "genuine awakening," as "life itself," as "full awareness," as something that can only be "pointed to," as something beyond dualities and beyond the reach of verbalization, is to use a language that would be recognized as Zen even by the most casual student of this Japanese approach to reality. Aldhelm Cameron-Brown has written of *New Seeds:* ". . . A suspicion which has been growing throughout the book is verified at the end, when Basho's frog plops onto the last page and we realize that Thomas Merton has come under the influence of Zen." Indeed he has; and when, in 1965, he wrote the preface to the Japanese edition of *Seeds of Contemplation,* he highlights his affinity with the monks of Zen: "The author of this book can say that he feels closer to the Zen monks of ancient Japan than to the busy impatient men of the West."

NEW THOUGHT ON CONTEMPLATION.* Merton begins *New Seeds* with an entirely new chapter, entitled "What Is Contemplation." The title strikes a familiar note: it recalls Merton's earliest writing on the subject of contemplation—the brief work he had produced in response to a theology student's request for an answer to the question that became the title of that earlier work and has now become the title of the initial chapter of *New Seeds.* One can suspect that Merton was less confident in 1962 that he could give an adequate answer to this question than he had been in 1948 when he sent to St. Mary's School of Theology, with permission to publish, the booklet *What Is Contemplation.*

In the booklet of 1948, Merton had written about the Roman Catholic tradition on the topic of contemplation, as one might find the tradition expressed in any standard manual of spiritual or mystical theology. It is an essentialist approach to contemplation, defining it in terms of the call to contemplation inherent in baptism and distinguishing it into infused contemplation and active contemplation, the former alone being contemplation in the strict sense.

In *New Seeds,* Merton is writing out of the background of that tradition, but describing contemplation in such a way that much of what he says could be understood and accepted by people belonging to other religious traditions. In no sense does he abandon the Western Christian tradition on the contemplative experience. (Many of the descriptive

---

*The new material on contemplation may be found in Chapters 1 and 2 (which are completely new), additions to Chapter 38, and Chapter 39 (also new), as well as in scattered corrections and additions throughout the text.

statements in Chapter 1 are distinctly Christian. Moreover, there is a large section of new material, in Chapter 21, on the importance of the humanity of Christ to the Christian contemplative.) But he considerably expands the perimeters of that experience. He had come to realize that contemplation, far from being a Catholic monopoly, is an experience that is shared by many religious traditions. Indeed, he was, more and more, prepared to say that other religious traditions—e.g., the Christian East and some of the religions of Asia—may well have been more faithful to the contemplative dimension of life than the Christian West, with its accent on action and material progress. His widening contact with the religions of Asia, notably Buddhism, gave him not only a deep respect for the mystical elements of these religions but also a new vocabulary to describe the experience of contemplation. *New Seeds* is an effort to harmonize the vocabulary of Western mystical literature, and some of its more modern expressions, with the vocabulary of other religious traditions; and the harmony is convincing.

The first chapter of *New Seeds,* though relatively brief, abounds in statements descriptive of the contemplative experience, any one of which the unwary reader might be tempted to take as a definition of contemplation. But in spite of what Grayston calls "his inveterate tendency in this direction," Merton does not intend these statements as definitions. They are different ways of attempting to express what in reality is undefinable.

He begins by describing contemplation as a state of heightened consciousness—an insight that would be congenial to most any contemplative tradition. "Contemplation," he writes, "is the highest expression of man's intellectual and spiritual life. It is that life itself, fully awake, fully active, fully aware that it is alive." One is reminded of Evelyn Underhill's statement: "Only the mystic can be called a whole man, since in others half the powers of the self always sleep."

This heightened consciousness does not mean being conscious of a particular object of perception; rather, it is pure consciousness, which Merton describes in a variety of ways: "spontaneous awe of the sacredness of life, of being"; "gratitude for life, for awareness and for being"; a breakthrough to a new level of reality: vivid awareness of the reality of the Source of life and being; "an awakening to the Real within all that is real."

The language of Zen and Christian mysticism vie with one another as Merton continues to pile description upon description. "Contemplation is the experience of the transcendent and inexpressible God." It is being touched by Him who has no hands; yet the "touch" is real, for it is "felt" at the very roots of our limited being. It is being called by Him who has no voice, yet whose word is heard in the depths of our heart. For we are words who respond to Him or, rather, who echo the word He speaks in us. And as an echo is not really distinct from the word whose resonance it is, so contemplation is a deep resonance in the inmost center of our spirit in which our very life "loses its separate voice" and resounds the word He speaks in us. "Contemplation is the awareness and realization, even in some sense *experience,* of what each Christian obscurely believes: 'It is now no longer I that live, but Christ lives in me.' " "It is awakening, enlightenment, the amazing intuitive grasp by which love gains certitude of God's creative and dynamic intervention in our daily life." "It is being carried away by Him into His own realm, His own mystery and His own freedom."

Yet when all the descriptions have been made and all the analogies drawn, one must say: But nothing of all this can tell you what contemplation truly is. For contemplation is an experience that is rich in meaning but "poor in concepts and poorer still in reasoning." No description or analogy can begin to convey the reality of the experience, for it is "too deep to be grasped in images, in words or even in clear concepts."

> It can be suggested by words, by symbols, but in the very moment of trying to indicate what it knows, the contemplative mind takes back what it has said and denies what it has affirmed. For in contemplation we know by "unknowing." Or better, we know *beyond* all knowing and "unknowing."

The reality of contemplation cannot be expressed in kataphatic terms alone. In the very act of saying that it is "this," one must, with equal emphasis, assert that it is "not this." Indeed, it is beyond "this" and "not this." Chapter 1, "What Is Contemplation," necessarily spills over into Chapter 2, "What Contemplation Is Not."

> For contemplation is always beyond our own knowledge, beyond our own light, beyond systems, beyond explanations, beyond discourse, beyond dialogue, beyond our own self.

The message of Merton's affirmations and negations is clear. He is not saying: If you do "this" and "this," you will probably become a contemplative. Rather, he is saying: If you are a contemplative, you will probably understand what I am saying; for probably some of the things I have said will already have happened to you. But what actually has happened to you is beyond your words or mine to express. No amount of verbalization can ever capture the experience of contemplation and make it intelligible to one who has not had it.

One who does not actually know, in his own life, the nature of this breakthrough and this awakening to a new level of reality cannot help being misled by most of the things that are said about it.

NEW THOUGHTS ON THE TRUE SELF.* The discovery of one's true identity is a major theme in Merton's writings on contemplation. We have seen in *Seeds* and in *The Inner Experience* how he develops this theme in terms of the disappearance of the false external self, which is ultimately illusory, and the emergence of the true self—the self we are before God.

In *New Seeds,* Merton identifies the external self with the "individual" or the "ego," and the true self with the "person." In doing so, he was probably influenced by Jacques Maritain, a longtime friend who on one occasion visited him at Gethsemani and with whom he corresponded with some frequency.†

In *Scholasticism and Politics,* which discusses at some length the difference between the individual and the person, Maritain writes: "Pascal tells us that 'the ego is hateful.' " "[This] is a commonplace expression of Pascalian literature . . . As a counterpart of the word of Pascal, we must remember the words of St. Thomas: 'The person is that which is noblest in the whole of nature.' "

---

*The new material on the self may be found in Chapters 2, 4, 6, 38, 39, and in scattered corrections and additions throughout the text.

†In a letter written to Maritain the year following the publication of *New Seeds,* Merton speaks of his personal struggle with the illusion of the false self: "Dear Jacques, you are going on your journey to God, and perhaps I am too, though I suppose my eagerness to go is partly wishful thinking, for there is yet work to be done in my own life. There are great illusions to be got rid of, and there is a false self that has to be taken off, if it can be done. There is still much change before I can really be living in the truth and in nothingness and in humility and without any self concern" (Letter of June 11, 1963, unpublished, in files of the Merton Studies Center, Louisville, Ky.).

This contrast between the "ego as hateful" and the person as that which is "noblest in nature" strikes responsive chords in *New Seeds*. Thus, Merton writes:

> The person must be rescued from the individual.* The free son of God must be saved from the conformist slave of fantasy, passion and convention. The creative and mysterious inner self must be delivered from the wasteful, hedonistic and destructive ego that seeks only to cover itself with disguises.†

Merton is telling us that freedom and reality reside, not in the individual, but in the person. Insofar as he is an individual, man is a "slave," in bondage to his own illusions and fantasies and victimized by his self-seeking, hedonistic, and ultimately destructive drives and desires. He is not just a "slave" but a "conformist slave," submitting blindly to material forces and to the conventions of the collective society in which he finds himself. The individual cannot function in community; instead, he escapes into "the great formless sea of irresponsibility which is the crowd." The collectivity swallows him up in its "shapeless and faceless

---

*While adopting the language of Maritain's Christian personalism that distinguishes the person from the individual, Merton does not abandon the terminology of his earlier writings. He continues to speak of the "true self" and the "external self."

†In a letter to Maritain dated May 24, 1964, Merton comments on the Buddhist doctrine of *anatta,* which is generally taken to mean a denial of person. He suggests that it may actually offer us new insights into the meaning of person. "I think that one of the most crucially important subjects to investigate today is the Buddhist metaphysic of the 'person' which claims to be non-personal *(anatta),* but as a matter of fact might well be something completely unique and challenging. The *anatta* idea is simply a 'no' to the Hindu *atman* as a pseudo-object of thought. If once one can find that, on this crucial point where Buddhism and Christianity are completely opposed, they are in fact perhaps united . . . Today is the feast of the Trinity. Person but not individual nature . . ." (Letter of May 24, 1964, unpublished, in the files of the Thomas Merton Studies Center, Louisville, Ky.).

mass." He may live in the midst of others, but is always apart from them, for he shares neither communion nor real communication but only "the common noise and the general distraction." Even when the individual seeks solitude, it is for the wrong reason: he seeks to escape from other people. For the individual does not know that "reality is to be sought not in division, but in unity." Solitude, therefore, becomes for him simply a refuge, a retreat from others. "The man who lives in division is not a person, but only an individual."

This is the individual: the slave self, the self that lives by illusion and in separateness. How very different the person! For, insofar as one is a person, he is free: he is a creative and mysterious center of freedom, unity, and independence, with a reality that is inviolate, eternal, and united to God. The person acts in community, able to share with others something that is truly personal and real, because he himself is real. The person separates himself from others in solitude, not to escape from them, but to find perspective —so that in interior silence he can learn to love not only God but also others and thus fulfill what is the noblest capacity of his nature. Merton writes:

> The person is constituted by a uniquely subsisting capacity to love—by a radical ability to care for all beings made by God and loved by Him. Such a capacity is destroyed by the loss of perspective.

Solitude gives that perspective. Whereas the individual seeks a false solitude that separates, the person seeks true solitude which unites in love. "True solitude is the home of the person, false solitude the refuge of the individualist."

Merton warns us, however, that in distinguishing the individual from the person we must avoid the Platonic error of identifying the individual with the body and the person with the soul. The person is not a part of ourselves: it is our whole reality.

> Hence both body and soul belong to, or better, subsist in our real self, the person that we are. The ego, on the other hand, is a self-constructed illusion that "has" our body and part of our soul at its disposal, because it has "taken over" the functions of the inner self as a result of what we call man's fall.

Essential for understanding Merton's distinction between the true self and the false self is an appreciation of the meaning he gives to the fall. The fall as he sees it—and in this he is following the teaching of the Greek Fathers—is a fall from unity into disunity, from depths into superficiality, from union with God into a state of alienation from Him. Because of the fall, our outer self masks our inner self, so that we do not know who we are. The only way we can return to unity in our own being and to communion with God is through contemplation. "The deep, transcendent self," Merton writes, "awakens only in contemplation." Apart from contemplation, we can discover our true self only in heaven. This is the destiny of many. "Most of us," Merton says, never discover "that mysterious and unknown self" until we are dead.

The return to God and the discovery of our identity in Him demand a long journey; and we have to start from where we are: our fallen state, our condition of alienation.

> We are prodigals in a distant country, "the region of unlikeness," and we must seem to travel far in that region before we reach our own land (and yet secretly we are in our own land all the time!).

The parenthesis in the above quotation is significant. The true self is not something we have to create. It is there as

God's gift to us. We have to awaken it, become aware of it. We have to discover that in the depths of our being we are contemplatives. In the meantime, accepting our existential situation as we are, we have to allow the "ego," the "outer self," to carry out the functions which our inner self cannot yet assume on its own. "We have to act in our everyday life as if we were what our outer self indicates us to be." Yet at the same time we must remember that what for the moment seems to be most real in us is actually a mask that covers what is truly real. Though we must adapt ourselves to our alienated condition, we can never rest comfortable with it.

At this point in our discussion of Merton's understanding of the external self, an important qualification must be made. "We must not," Merton says, "deal in too negative a fashion with the external self." This is precisely what we have done thus far: for we have considered passages in which Merton views the external self in a pejorative way: it is the false self that alienates us from God and from our own inner unity: the "hateful ego" of Pascal; the self that ultimately is a lie. It is from this external self, considered as the *false* self, that we must be delivered. But, paradoxically, this very external self may initiate our deliverance. For there is another way of viewing the external self. While Merton generally describes it in pejorative terms, there are passages in *New Seeds* (and elsewhere in his writings) where his descriptions are more neutral than pejorative. The external self is presented at times not as false but simply as superficial. It is frail. It is feeble. Granted these are hardly words of praise; but neither are they words of condemnation. What is frail and feeble deserves, at the very least, our sympathy. What is superficial may be on the threshold of a breakthrough to what is below the surface. Merton speaks of such a breakthrough:

When I consent to the will and mercy of God as it "comes" to me in the events of life, appealing to my inner self and awakening my faith, I break through the superficial exterior appearances that form my routine vision of the world and of my own self, and I find myself in the presence of hidden majesty.

The superficial self is the self that lives at the level of appearances. While appearances are never a substitute for reality, "they can be transparent media in which we apprehend the presence of God in the world."

> It is possible to speak of the exterior self as a mask: to do so is not necessarily to reprove it. The mask that each man wears may well be a disguise not only for that man's inner self but for God, wandering as a pilgrim and exile in His own creation.

Apprehending the Creator as a pilgrim in His own world may well be the door that opens the way to the contemplative experience, in which we move from a knowledge of God disguised in the world of things to an experience of Him as He is in Himself. At this point, the inner self is at last able to assume its own function. Then "God confronts man not through the medium of things," but in His own simplicity.

> The union of the simple light of God with the simple light of man's spirit, in love, is contemplation . . . In this meeting there is not so much a fusion of identities as a disappearance of identities.

God raises us above dualities and makes us one with Him. Our subjectivity becomes one with the subjectivity of God.

> For in the depths of contemplative prayer there seems to be no division between subject and object, and there is no reason to make any statement either about God or about oneself. HE IS and His reality absorbs everything else.

NEW THOUGHTS ON FAITH.* In *The Ascent to Truth,* Merton had made it clear that faith is more than intellectual assent to propositions and concepts about God. For faith not only attains to God as He is revealed in the articles of faith, it attains to God Himself who reveals; that is, to God as He really is, but known in the darkness of unknowing.

In *New Seeds,* Merton reiterates this perspective on faith and expands it. Faith is intellectual assent, but it is more; it is the whole person assenting not merely to truths about God but also, and especially, to God Himself. In faith, one not only "hears" God, he "receives God." For the propositions which faith accepts on divine authority are media through which we grasp God, or, better still, are grasped by Him. Faith, therefore, terminates, not in statements or formulas, but in God Himself. For this reason the formulas of faith are not ends in themselves; rather, they are means whereby God communicates Himself to us. While we must make every effort to express the content of faith in precise formulas, "we must not be so obsessed with verbal correctness that we never go beyond the words to the ineffable reality which they attempt to convey . . . For faith is the opening of an inward eye, the eye of the heart, to be filled with the presence of Divine light." This Divine light, however, as Merton makes clear in *The Ascent to Truth,* is so dazzling that it is darkness for us: we apprehend God in "the darkness of faith."

Because faith is adherence to what we do not see, the act of faith, as Merton pointed out in *The Ascent to Truth,* is elicited under the impulsion of the will. In the act of faith we submit to authority as it teaches us what God has revealed. But Merton warns in *New Seeds* that submission to authority which proposes the truths of revelation must not

*See especially Chapters 18, 19, 25.

be "so overemphasized that it seems to constitute the whole essence of faith." Faith must not be reduced to an act of obedience. Such reductionism could lead to a credulity that revels in the unintelligible, as in the case of the person who said of the Trinity: "Wish there were four of them, so that I might believe in more of them." Reducing faith to obedience could well strip faith of any real content. It could also lead to "a forced suppression of doubt rather than an opening of the eye of the heart by deep belief." Doubts about faith need to be faced and dealt with, not suppressed. Most often, they do not indicate an unwillingness or an inability on our part to accept the propositions of faith but simply a sense of our weakness and helplessness in the presence of the awful mystery of God.

In faith I not only encounter God, I also encounter myself in the mystery of my life at a level beyond concepts and rationalization. Faith opens up new dimensions of our being, integrating in the unity of the person the unknown that is below reason with the unknown that is above reason. That is to say, faith serves as a principle of integration, bringing together into one whole the unconscious (the realm of instinct and emotion that is below reason), the conscious (the realm of intelligence and thought), and the superconscious (the realm that is beyond reason's ken). The Greek Fathers used three terms to describe these dimensions of the human person: the unconscious they called *anima* (in Greek, *psyche*); the conscious principle, *animus* (in Greek, *nous*); and that which integrates both, *spiritus* (*pneuma*, in Greek). *Anima*, the feminine principle, is Eve; *animus*, the masculine principle, is Adam.* The meaning of Original Sin is that Eve tempts Adam and he falls into a

---

*This is not "sexist" language (though one need not deny that the Greek Fathers used such language in other contexts!); it is in this instance the language of myth.

state in which reasoned activity continually yields to the movement of blind impulse and emotion.

Faith restores the proper balance in one's life, not simply by achieving the submission of instinct to reason, but by transcending both and integrating them into a higher principle which is "above the division of masculine and feminine, active and passive, prudential and instinctive." This higher principle is *spiritus,* or *pneuma,* of which St. Paul writes: "If you are guided by the Spirit, you will not fulfill the desires of your lower nature."

> The "spiritual life" is then the perfectly balanced life in which the body with its passions and instincts, the mind with its reasoning and its obedience to principle, and the spirit with its passive illumination by the Light and Love of God form one complete man who is in God and with God and from God and for God. One man in whom God is all in all. One man in whom God carries out His own will without obstacle.

Such a person, living by faith and united with God in the Spirit, is the true self. It is the contemplative person.

VII

The Climate of Monastic Prayer
(Contemplative Prayer)

In 1964 Thomas Merton wrote an article called "The Climate of Monastic Prayer." This article, at first privately circulated, was published in 1965 in *Collectanea Cisterciensia*. During the year 1965 Merton enlarged the article, originally fifteen pages, into a fifty-eight-page booklet that was completed in October 1965. This booklet, carrying the same title as the original article, was also privately circulated. Some time after October 1965, Merton expanded this booklet into a book, also titled *The Climate of Monastic Prayer,* which was published in 1969 by Cistercian Publications. (The identical text, but with different page numbering, was published the same year by Herder and Herder under another title, *Contemplative Prayer.* The book contains 126 pages of Merton material and a preface of fifteen pages written by Merton's friend, Dr. Douglas V. Steere.)

An intelligent reading of this book requires some understanding of the way in which Merton expanded the booklet of October 1965 into a book. He did so, not by writing new material, but by inserting (one is tempted to say intruding) at various points into the booklet *verbatim* excerpts from an unpublished manuscript of his called *Prayer as Worship and Experience*. This manuscript, offered originally in 1963 to Macmillan Company for publication and withdrawn that same year, is made up of four sections: I. The Life of Prayer; II. Prayer as Worship; III. Prayer as Experience; and IV. Epilogue: Wisdom or Evasion. It was the last two sections of this unpublished manuscript which Merton inserted into the booklet to create the book. Diagram (C), on the following page, shows how Merton combined the primary material of the book—namely, the booklet of October 1965—with the secondary material—namely, the third and fourth sections of *Prayer as Worship and Experience.*

This diagram is not intended to be an idle exercise in "source criticism"; it is considered by the writer an essential tool for any enlightened reading of *The Climate of Monastic Prayer.* It is necessary, for example, for the reader to know that there is a continuity between Chapter V of the book, which concludes with some remarks on the "purpose of monastic prayer . . . in the sense of prayer of the heart," and Chapter XI, which begins with the question: "What is the purpose of meditation, in the sense of 'the prayer of the heart'?" Between these two chapters there is a huge parenthesis—five chapters and twenty-seven pages long—which discusses the history of private prayer in the Benedictine tradition from the time of St. Benedict to the Counter-Reformation and after. Following this parenthetical intrusion, Merton returns in Chapter XI to the topic he had been discussing in Chapter V. To understand what Merton is doing, it is necessary for the reader to know that the long historical digression which he inserts at this point actually comes from another source and was not written with this book in mind at all.

The same may be said about Chapters XII and XIII and

Diagram C: THE CLIMATE OF MONASTIC PRAYER

THE BOOK	THE BOOKLET (OCT. 1965)	PRAYER AS WORSHIP AND EXPERIENCE
Introduction (pp. 29–38)	Introduction (pp. 1–6)	
Ch. I (39–41)	Ch. I (1–2)	
Ch. II (42–48)	Ch. II (1–4)	
Ch. III (49–53)	Ch. III (1–4)	
Ch. IV (54–59)	Ch. IV (1–8)	Part III Prayer as Experience
Ch. V (60–64)		1. Mental Prayer and Contemplation
Ch. VI (65–69)		Personal Prayer in the Benedictine Tradition (pp. 87–89)
Ch. VII (70–74)		St. Gregory the Great (89–92)
Ch. VIII (75–79)		St. Bernard of Clairvaux (92–95)
Ch. IX and initial paragraphs of Ch. X (80–85)		
		Peter of Celles (95–98)
Ch. X (remainder) (85–91)		
		Benedictine Prayer in the Counter-Reformation and After (98–102)
Ch. XI (92–98)	Ch. V (1–6)	
Ch. XII (99–102)		Ascetic Purification (106–8)
Ch. XIII (103–7)		Passive Purification (108–11)
Ch. XIV (108–20)	Ch. VI (1–11)	
Ch. XV (121–29)		2. The Way of Contemplative Prayer (111–16)
Ch. XVI (130–38)	Ch. VII (1–8)	
Ch. XVII (139–40)	Ch. VIII (1–2)	
Ch. XVIII (141–48)	Ch. IX (1–7)	
Ch. XIX		Part IV Epilogue: Wisdom or Evasion (117–22)

CLIMATE OF MONASTIC PRAYER
Douglas V. Steere: Foreword: 15 pp.
Total Merton Material: 126 pp.
(75 pp. from booklet of October 1965
51 pp.: excerpts from *Prayer as Worship and Experience*)

Chapter XV: they are insertions into the text which do not blend harmoniously with the original material of the book.

From the diagram and from the brief remarks just made about it, it can be readily seen that what we are dealing with in *The Climate of Monastic Prayer* is actually two books, one within the other, or, perhaps more accurately, the second scattered through the first. The "primary material," taken from the October 1965 booklet, comprises seventy-five pages of the text. The "book within the book," the "secondary material" from *Prayer as Worship and Experience,* makes up the other fifty-one pages. The reader would be well advised to read the text as two separate books. This would mean reading ten chapters (seventy-five pages) as *The Climate of Monastic Prayer* and nine chapters (fifty-one pages) as a totally different work.* This is the approach to the text that the writer intends to follow in this summary. He will summarize first the "primary material" and then the "secondary material."† He is persuaded that this dual path through the text will make the study of the book much more intelligible.

As has been mentioned, the book under discussion was published under two different titles: *The Climate of Monastic Prayer* (Cistercian Publications edition) and *Contemplative Prayer* (the Herder and Herder edition). The choice of the title *Contemplative Prayer* for the Herder and Herder publication was obviously intended to open the book to a wider readership by suggesting through the new title that the book would be of interest to people who were not monks. Merton states in his introduction:

---

*The first "book" would include Chapters I–V, XI, XIV, XVI, XVII, XVIII; the second "book," Chapters VI, VII, VIII, IX, X, XII, XIII, XV, XIX.

†By "primary material," the writer intends to designate the contents of the booklet of October 1965; by "secondary material," the excerpts from *Prayer as Worship and Experience.*

What is written about prayer in these pages is written primarily for monks. However . . . a practical, non-academic study of monastic prayer should be of interest to all Christians, since every Christian is bound to be in some sense a man of prayer.

Merton had apparently expressed, in a letter to Mrs. Naomi Burton Stone, his concern that some revisions in the book were called for to make it more appealing to a general readership. For, on March 8, 1966, Mrs. Stone wrote to him:

> I have nearly finished reading *The Climate of Monastic Prayer* and think it's terrific! Obviously, as you say, it will need more revision for the general public, but I think that the general public can get a great deal out of it.

Actually, very little revision was made in the original text to accommodate the book to the needs of the "general public." Apart from the change in title in the Herder and Herder edition and the occasional substitution of "prayer" for "monastic prayer," the book remains in its original form. Merton may have considered the insertion of the "secondary material" from the unpublished manuscript as an accommodation to a more general public; but in view of the confusion which this material introduced into the book, as well as the largely "monastic" character of the insertions themselves, it can be doubted that this secondary material actually helped in any way to make the book appeal to a wider readership.

The book remains, in other words, what it was originally intended to be: a book for monks. This is not to say that it has nothing to offer to people who are not monks. Much that Merton says about monastic prayer can be adapted with great profit to the life of the lay Christian; but he has to make that adaption on his own. Merton has made only token gestures in that direction. The book remains *The Climate of MONASTIC Prayer.* In fact, one might seriously question whether the substitution of *Contemplative Prayer* for the original title is accurate or justifiable. The term "contemplative prayer" occurs only six times in the text: five times in the "secondary material"* and only once in the "primary material."† (Even the word "contemplation" is used only sparingly in the "primary material.) The word Merton seems to prefer in this book to describe monastic prayer is, curiously, the word "meditation." (Interestingly, on page 150, in the midst of a section from the "secondary material," Merton substitutes the word "meditation" for what was "prayer" in the original text of the unpublished manuscript.) He frequently uses "prayer of the heart" as a synonym for "meditation." Either of these two terms would have reflected the book's terminology more accurately than *Contemplative Prayer.*

THE PRIMARY MATERIAL. Merton identifies the climate of monastic prayer as the desert.

> The climate in which monastic prayer flowers is that of the desert, where the comfort of man is absent, where the secure routines of man's city offer no support, and where prayer must be sustained by God in the purity of faith.

The desert is the climate of monastic prayer both historically and existentially. Historically, it is the climate of monastic prayer because the desert is the place where monastic prayer originated. Specifically, it is the Egyptian desert where St. Anthony went to give up all things for the love and service of God, where others followed him in great numbers, and where John Cassian (*c.* 360–435) came to

---

*Pages 66, 76, 83, 121, 127.
†Page 56.

drink from its source the wisdom that these Desert Fathers had come to experience in their prayer.

Merton always had a deep affection for the Desert Fathers, "those men of fabulous originality" who "sought a way to God that was uncharted and freely chosen, not inherited from others who have mapped it out beforehand. They sought a God whom they alone could find, not one who was 'given' in a set stereotyped form by somebody else." They "did not imagine themselves to be mystics," Merton says, "though in fact they often were."

The key that opens the door to the spirituality of the Desert Fathers is the "heart." Their prayer was the "prayer of the heart." It was, first of all, the Bible in the heart. Their lives were rooted in the Scriptures, especially in the psalms. They were not biblical scholars: they did not analyze biblical texts. They put the Bible in their hearts by memorizing its words and repeating them with deep and simple concentration. The psalter was especially their book of prayer, for in the psalms they saw "revealed the secret movements of the heart in its struggle against the forces of darkness. The 'battle psalms' were all interpreted as referring to the war with passion and with the demons."

Their prayer was also "Jesus in the heart." "The Prayer of Jesus," so popular in the Eastern Church, originated in the Egyptian desert. It "consisted in interior recollection, the abandonment of distracting thoughts, and the humble invocation of the Lord Jesus with words from the Bible in a spirit of intense faith." Keeping the name of Jesus in the ground of their being was for them the secret of the control of thoughts and of victory over temptation. It was the way of keeping themselves in the presence of God and in touch with the reality of their own inner truth. They could find God in their lives only if they were in touch with their own inner truth; and they could experience their own true selves only if they were truly in the presence of God. This was the reason they had come into the desert: "to be themselves, their ordinary selves, and to forget a world that divided them from themselves" and separated them from God.

The ultimate goal of their lives was the kingdom of God and union with Him; but the proximate goal to which they directed all their energies was "purity of heart," which is the aim of "prayer of the heart." Purity of heart meant for them much more than moral or even ascetical perfection. It was the culmination of a long process of spiritual transformation whereby, detached from all creatures and freed from all movement of inordinate passion, they were able to live "absorbed in God." Purity of heart meant "keeping their minds and hearts empty of care and concern, so that they might altogether forget themselves and apply themselves entirely to the love and service of God."

They did not talk a great deal about purity of heart. They lived and experienced it; and from their experience they distilled a very practical and unassuming wisdom that shines through the words they spoke that have been preserved for us. This wisdom represents a discovery of the reality of the human person in the course of an inner and spiritual journey that, as Merton says, "is far more crucial and infinitely more important than any journey to the moon." "What," he asks, "can we gain by sailing to the moon if we are not able to cross the abyss that separates us from ourselves?"

The climate of monastic prayer is not only the desert historically; it is also the desert in an existential sense: it is the solitude of the monk in which he seeks the ground of his own being, searching his own heart and plunging into the heart of the world, of which he is after all a part, in order that he may listen more attentively to the deepest and more neglected voices that proceed from the depths of what is most truly real. "The monk," Merton says, "is bound to explore the inner waste of his own being as a solitary," with an ever "deepening existential grasp of his call to life in Christ." This means for today's monk what it meant for the early Desert Fathers: breaking with the familiar and established and secure norms to travel off into the unknown toward a freedom rooted not in social approval but in a profound sense of dependence on God in pure faith. To achieve this freedom, the monk must first endure the questioning and the doubt and the sense of dread that will force him to confront his false self with its illusions, its masks, and its role playing. As Merton puts it:

> The dimensions of prayer in solitude are those of man's ordinary anguish, his self-searching, his moments of nausea at his own vanity, falsity and capacity for betrayal. Far from establishing one in unassailable narcissistic security, the way of prayer brings us face to face with the sham and indignity of the false self that seeks to live for itself and to enjoy the "consolations of prayer" for its own sake. This self is pure illusion and ultimately he who lives for and by such an illusion must end either in disgust or madness.

It is only by unmasking this false self in the solitude of prayer that the monk can be delivered from the bondage of an inauthentic existence and hope to recover a sense of his true self firmly rooted in his own inner truth. "The monk confronts his own humanity at the deepest and most central point where the void seems to enter into black despair." He faces the serious possibility that despair may be the only answer to life's ambiguities; and he rejects it. For in the darkness the firm stand he has taken, beyond falsity and illusion, in the ground of his being, opens to him the light of God by which he can perceive, however dimly, the mysterious workings of the Spirit of God who makes all things new and creates a new humanity in Christ.

This, then, is the climate of monastic prayer: the desert of Egypt and the lonely waste of the monk's own solitude. Both are "places" where he comes to realize that he is not at home in the world and that the world by itself can offer him no ultimate meaning for the life he lives in it. This ultimate meaning, which the world cannot give, is something that the monk discovers only when he transcends his own humanity and that of the world by a freedom that turns despair into hope and a life of illusion into a life of authentic existence. Become at last aware of God, he lets his heart go out in gratitude, obedient love, and service to the One who has enabled him to know his inner truth. "The climate of this prayer is, then, one of awareness, gratitude and a totally obedient love which seeks nothing but to please God."

This book is about monastic prayer. In it Merton discusses prayer in its very nature rather than its techniques. While he draws occasionally on ancient texts, "the whole development," Merton states, "is essentially modern." For a contemporary understanding of meditation (i.e., "prayer in the heart," or prayer in the ground of one's being), Merton turns not only to the Egyptian Fathers but also to modern existentialists, with their emphasis on freedom and the human need for authenticity and spiritual liberation, with their exploration of the dark side of the human psyche in terms of the ineluctable fact of death and the sense of dread in the face of the apparent meaninglessness of life. There are explicit references to Heidegger and Marcel and implicit references to Kierkegaard's important work, *The Concept of Dread.*

Merton's study of monastic prayer is concerned especially with personal prayer, although in the "secondary material" of the book he does discuss the relationship of personal prayer to liturgy and to a life of action. His special concern, in discussing prayer, is "the monk's own deepening existential grasp of his call to life in Christ, as it progressively reveals itself to him in the solitude where he is alone with God."

The prayer life of the monk is richer than any particular "spiritual exercise." Meditation, psalmody, prayerful reading of the Scriptures *(lectio divina),* and contemplation are all part of a unified and integrated life in which the monk turns from the world to God. Monastic prayer is, therefore, the ensemble of these varied ways of finding God and resting in His presence.

Though he uses in his title the words "monastic prayer," Merton's emphasis throughout the book is on the "meditation" of the monk. He makes it clear that he wants to understand meditation in its close relation to psalmody, reading, prayer, and contemplation, yet he scarcely touches on meditation's relationship to these other important aspects of monastic prayer.

Merton's concentration in this book on the "meditation" of the monk is, to say the least, curious. One would expect, in the light of his previous books, that in writing about the central exercise of monastic prayer he would have chosen to discuss the "contemplation" of the monk; yet, as was pointed out above in the "primary material" of the book, the word "contemplation" occurs only infrequently and the words "contemplative prayer" only once. Why does he use the word "meditation," when his preferred term for the life of prayer, as evidenced by his earlier works, is "contemplation"?

Did he perhaps use the word "meditation" because, at the time he wrote, meditation as a practice borrowed from

Hinduism and Buddhism was enjoying a wide popularity in the West among Christians and non-Christians alike? Was he perhaps intending to point out to those who were embracing this practice in large numbers that it is more than a psychological exercise that may bring a measure of quiet and a power of concentration into a person's life; that it was a deeply spiritual experience that can change the whole orientation of a person's life? Was he perhaps trying to show that meditation need not be an import from the East, but was actually a practice deeply rooted in the Christian tradition of prayer?

Whatever may have been Merton's reason for using the word "meditation" rather than "contemplation" to describe the central reality of monastic spirituality, it should be made clear that in this book he gives a very precise meaning to the term "meditation." By meditation he does not mean "mental prayer," which, he says, "is totally misleading in the monastic context. We rarely pray with the mind alone." Mental prayer suggests a cleavage between prayer in the mind and vocal prayer—something totally foreign to any understanding of the monastic life. Nor does he mean "discursive meditation," which consists of "busy discursive acts, complex logical reasoning, active imagining, and the deliberate stirring up of the affections." Meditation in this sense, Merton believes, tends to conflict with our receptivity to the inner working of the Holy Spirit. While it is true that discursive meditation can serve a valid purpose in the Christian life, one needs to know, as Merton has pointed out in other works, when its usefulness for spiritual growth has come to an end and therefore when it should be abandoned for a way of prayer that, even though it may be more obscure, will be more fruitful.

By meditation, Merton means a type of prayer that has some kinship with authentic Zen meditation in that it seeks an intuition of being beyond the dualities of life. Like Zen, it is an integrating prayer in which one finds the center of his life, his "original self" (as Zen practitioners would put it). It differs, however, from Zen in that Merton would see that center as rooted in God.

Perhaps the best way of understanding what Merton wants to express by the term "meditation" is to link it with the prayer of the early Desert Fathers. In fact, Merton explicitly does this. He says:

> In these pages meditation will be used as more or less equivalent to what mystics of the Eastern Church have called "prayer of the heart"—at least in its general sense of prayer that seeks its roots in the very ground of our being, not merely in our mind or our affections.

Again he writes:

> Monastic prayer begins not so much with "considerations" as with a "return to the heart," finding one's deepest center, awakening the profound depths of our being and our life.

Merton clarifies what he means by the "heart" and "the return to the heart." The heart, he says, is "the deepest psychological ground of one's personality,"

> the inner sanctuary where self-awareness goes beyond analytical reflection and opens out into metaphysical and theological confrontation with the Abyss of the unknown yet present—one who is "more intimate to us than we are to ourselves."

"Return to the heart" means that "purity of heart"—so important to the Desert Fathers—which is the only atmosphere in which the "prayer of the heart" can grow and flourish. "Purity of heart" involves total surrender to God as the Source and Ground of our being and an unconditional acceptance of our situation as willed by Him. It is an existential acceptance of the whole of reality, seen at once in its depths and in its concreteness.

Some people have a spontaneous gift for meditation; others enter upon the experience only with difficulty. Most of us have to learn how to meditate. Yet, learning how to meditate means not so much looking for a "method" or a "system" as cultivating an "outlook," an "attitude": faith, submission, attention, expectation, supplication, trust, and joy. Such attitudes will permeate our being with love and living faith that will help us to experience the presence of God, seeing Him without "seeing," knowing Him without "knowing."

We need to realize, too, that there is a movement in prayer. It is the rhythm of the paschal mystery: the passage from life to death, the alternation of darkness and light. Sometimes meditation is death and darkness; a descent into our nothingness, a recognition of our helplessness, our dependency, our sinfulness. But at other times we pierce through the darkness, as God leads us by the light of faith into new realms, wherein we become increasingly receptive to the hidden action of the Holy Spirit and begin to realize that God is All.

At times the darkness we experience in our prayer may be God's work in our lives, calling us to greater detachment and to a more obedient and cooperative submission to His grace. It may be God's grace "emptying our minds and hearts of the connatural satisfactions of knowledge and love on a simply human plane," in order to fill them "with the higher and purer light of faith which is 'darkness' to sense and reason." This is the "dark night" of which St. John of the Cross speaks—a night in which God darkens the mind only in order to give a more perfect light. It is excessive light that causes the darkness.

Yet we must not overlook the possibility that the darkness we encounter in meditation may be of our own making. It may be brought on by the false dichotomy we set up between the world of inner truth and the world of external realities—a dichotomy that prevents us from accepting the whole of reality for what it is. For meditation is not an exploration of abstract ideals; it must respect the concrete realities of everyday life—nature, the body, one's work, one's friends, one's surroundings. In a passage which suggests the influence of Zen and its "pointing" to the concrete realities of ordinary life as the way to enlightenment, Merton writes:

> A false supernaturalism which imagines that the "Supernatural" is a kind of Platonic realm of abstract essences totally apart from and opposed to the concrete world of nature offers no real support to a genuine life of meditation and prayer. Meditation has no point and no reality unless it is firmly rooted in *life*.

Meditation cannot be a "privatized" experience. We are not really progressing in meditation if we wall ourselves up inside ourselves in order to cherish our thoughts and experiences as a kind of private treasure. Love for others and openness to them remains, as in the active life, "the condition for a living and fruitful inner life of thought and love. The love of others is a stimulus to interior life, not a danger to it, as some mistakenly believe."

This definite, though not always unambiguous, concern for the ordinary realities of life and for an openness to other people as necessary conditions for a genuine interior life represents a shift of emphasis in Merton's writings. One might want to suggest that such concern is at least latent in his earlier books; but there can scarcely be any doubt that his explicit articulation of it in this book bears the mark of his contact with Zen Buddhism.

THE PURPOSE OF MEDITATION: (1) THE DISCOVERY OF WHO I AM. One of the goals of meditation is to answer the question: Who am I? Meditation seeks for the deepest ground of my identity in God's truth and in the realization of my total dependence on Him. Its goal is that purity of heart whereby I surrender myself to God and His purposes for me and in the process come to understand my own identity.

I am, Merton says, "a word spoken by God." God's words always have meaning; my task, therefore, is to discover the meaning that I am. What is the word God speaks in me? What is my identity? It is not an identity foisted upon me. The "word" (logos), as Merton understands it, is not the stoic notion of a meaning imposed on man from within by a static natural law; much less is it a meaning imposed on him from without by custom, routine, or social forces. It is, rather, a meaning that man is called by God to construct. "My true identity lies hidden in God's call to my freedom and my response to Him."

> This means I must use my freedom in order to *love,* with full responsibility and authenticity, not merely receiving a form imposed on me by external forces or forming my own life according to an approved social pattern, but directing my love to the personal reality of my brother, and embracing God's will in its naked, often unpenetrable mystery.

But I cannot discover my meaning in God till I realize how utterly void of meaning I am without Him. This experience of life's meaninglessness is dread. Hence Merton says: "I cannot discover my 'meaning' if I try to evade the dread which comes from first experiencing my meaninglessness."

My descent into the center of my being where I experience my nothingness before God must be authentic; that is to say, it must be genuinely lived by me. I cannot simply play a religious role. It is not enough for me to "believe" that I am grounded in God; I must experience it. We must let ourselves "be brought naked and defenseless into the center of that dread where we stand alone before God in our nothingness, without explanation, without theories, completely dependent upon His providential care, in dire need of the gift of His grace, His mercy and the light of faith."

This confrontation with our nothingness and helplessness is an experience of dread; yet this same confrontation *in the presence of God* is an experience of joy. For it puts us in "direct contact with the source of all joy and all life." In God we find our meaning. In Him we find our "heart." At the same time we unmask the false identity we had been living: we recognize that our external, everyday self is to a great extent a mask and a fabrication. In hiddenness and obscurity we come to know the true self that we are at our center. It is only then that we truly begin to meditate: for meditation cannot be the action of a false self.

THE PURPOSE OF MEDITATION: (2) THE DISCOVERY OF GOD AS HE IS. The goal of meditation is not only to know ourselves as we really are but also to know God as He is. To know God as He is can never mean knowing Him as an object that submits to our scrutiny. For God is not an "object" or a "thing." His infinity, as the very word implies, knows no boundaries; hence we cannot "define" Him as we define things in the world. "His presence cannot be verified as we would verify a laboratory experiment." As soon as we try to verify His presence as an object of exact knowledge, He eludes us.

The only knowledge of God of which we are capable is knowledge *about* Him—through analogies, images, and symbols. We must not underestimate the value of the conceptual knowledge of God that the imagery and symbols of our culture offer us. The richer this imagery, the more deeply will we be able to penetrate into the presence of God in His creation and the better prepared will our inner self be for the experience of God in faith. More than that, this imagery will enable one who has had the experience of God to reflect on that experience and articulate it for others.

But the true experience of God can never be achieved through our conceptual knowledge of Him. If we are to know Him as He is, we must transcend our analogies and "grasp" Him in the general awareness of loving faith, knowing Him by "unknowing." Indeed, we must not only transcend our analogies, we must also transcend our ordinary ways of knowing. "We must forget the familiar subject-object relationship" and "become aware of ourselves as known through and through by Him."

> Hence the aim of meditation, in the context of Christian faith, is not to arrive at an objective and apparently "scientific" knowledge about God, but to come to know Him through the realization that our very being is penetrated with His knowledge and love for us. Our knowledge of God is paradoxically a knowledge not of Him as the object of our scrutiny, but of ourselves as utterly dependent on His saving and merciful knowledge of us.

Thus, coming to know God in Himself and coming to know my real self converge in a single intuition—my awareness of my total dependence on Him. When I know Him, I know myself; when I know myself, I know Him. The goal of meditation is well summed up in the prayer of St. Augustine: *"Noverim te, noverim me"* ("May I know You, may I know myself").

Dread, or anxiety, is a condition of human existence that has been analyzed at great length by contemporary existentialists. Those who have written about it are careful to distinguish dread from fear. Fear always has some specific thing in the world as its object. When I fear, I know precisely what it is that I fear. Dread has no such specificity. It is the awakening of a person to the reality of an existence in which his freedom is poised over an abyss of nothingness. In his important book, *The Concept of Dread*, Sören Kierkegaard likens dread to the experience of dizziness.

> He whose eye chances to look down into the yawning abyss becomes dizzy . . . Thus dread is the dizziness of freedom which occurs . . . when freedom gazes down into its own possibility, grasping at finiteness to sustain itself.

It is only through experiencing this dread and coming to realize that finiteness cannot sustain him that one is able to break the bondage and the forgetfulness that tie him to "things in the world." Then he can begin to live an authentic life.

Merton links the existentialist's concept of dread with the "fear of the Lord" of the early Fathers and with the "dark nights" of St. John of the Cross. But he sees dread as more than a perception of our contingency, our finiteness, our ultimate "nothingness." For the poverty of our creatureliness is compounded by the fact that we are sinners alienated from God. We are not only creatures, we are creatures in rebellion. In our depths there is not only nothingness, there is also falsity. We have failed to measure up to the existential demands of our lives. We have failed to meet the challenge of our meaning as "words of God." And the price of this failure is guilt—a guilt that is real and not just a neurotic anxiety.

> It is the sense of defection and defeat that affects a man who is not facing his own inner truth and is not giving back to life, to God and to his fellow men a fair return for all that has been given him.

Dread is not simply a feeling of being out of favor with God. For estrangement from God can be juridically regained through receiving the sacraments of the Church with the proper dispositions. Indeed, one may do so and feel himself fully restored to the divine favor; "but this will not liberate him from 'dread' and 'night,' as long as he tends to cling to the empty illusion of a separate self, inclined to resist God." For dread, Merton says, is

> the deep, confused metaphysical awareness of a basic antagonism between the self and God due to estrangement from Him by perverse attachment to a self that is mysterious and illusory.

It is something that cannot be assigned to a definite cause or attributed to a specific action. It is not something we can repent of, but an experience we must face and struggle with.

Meditation is the scene of that struggle. The struggle ends at the moment we learn that we can find our authentic existence only when we are lost in God. It ends when we come to realize that we have no hope but in Him.

In the struggle we prove "the seriousness of our love for God and prayer," and in the peace that follows the struggle we come to realize that the experience of dread was not a punishment but a purification and a grace. Though the experience of it may have seemed a kind of hell, it turns out to be, in the words of the twelfth-century Cistercian, Isaac of Stella, "a hell of mercy and not of wrath." As Merton described it:

> To be in a "hell of mercy" is to fully experience one's nothingness, but in a spirit of repentance and surrender to God with desire to accept and do His will ... It is in this "hell of mercy" that, in finally relaxing our determined grasp of our empty self, we find ourselves lost and liberated in the

infinite fullness of God's love. We escape from the cage of emptiness, despair, dread and sin into the infinite space and freedom of grace and mercy.

THE SECONDARY MATERIAL. A substantive portion of the "secondary material" in *The Climate of Monastic Prayer* deals with the role of action and contemplation in the life of the monk. Merton presents in Chapters VI to X an historical perspective in which to place the discussion of these two aspects of monastic life.

BEFORE ST. BENEDICT. Out of the earliest monastic experience there emerged two divergent concepts of prayer: that of St. Anthony (251?–356) in the Egyptian desert and that of St. Basil (*c.* 330–379) at Annesi near Constantinople. St. Anthony represents an understanding of prayer that is essentially contemplative; St. Basil, one that is essentially active. For the Egyptian monks who followed St. Anthony, prayer meant resting as far as possible from exterior activity and seeking God in solitude. For the monastic communities founded by St. Basil, prayer is that which accompanies work and sanctifies it. Whereas the Egyptian monks saw contemplation in solitude as the heart of monastic prayer, St. Basil felt that such prayer was to be discouraged. He organized the prayer life of his monks according to the pattern of the canonical hours, leaving private prayer to be carried out by the monks while they were busy at the tasks assigned to them. "In the midst of our work," he said, "we can fulfill the duty of prayer."

The Rule of St. Benedict (*c.* 480–*c.* 550) provides for a balance of both liturgical prayer and contemplative prayer. Influenced by John Cassian (*c.* 360–435), the Rule expresses "the classical monastic belief that secret and contemplative prayer should be inspired by liturgical prayer and should be the normal crown of that prayer." In the early Benedictine tradition and in the spiritual writers of the Middle Ages, there is no conflict between "public" and "private" prayer or between liturgy and contemplation. This is a modern problem, or, as Merton suggests, a pseudo-problem. The Benedictine ideal was that

> liturgy by its very nature tends to prolong itself in individual contemplative prayer; and mental prayer in its turn disposes us for and seeks fulfillment in liturgical worship.

St. Gregory the Great. The problem that does arise in the Benedictine tradition is the problem of the relationship of the life of contemplation to the active life. St. Gregory the Great (*c.* 540–604) wrestled with the problem, and his treatment of it "has profoundly influenced Benedictine life in subsequent ages." Gregory's solution is that "the contemplative life is theoretically superior to and better than the active and should be preferred to the active whenever possible"; however, "there are times when activity must supplant contemplation." Hence, what is theoretically better may not necessarily be the choice one should make in a given situation. St. Gregory makes it clear, however, that the monk who is required by strict duty to leave contemplation for action should do so only with regret.

> The vocation of the monk was to stay in his monastery and pray, and when he was called forth from the cloister, as he often was, to engage in church affairs, he was expected to go forth with weeping and lamentation.

St. Bernard of Clairvaux. St. Bernard of Clairvaux (1090–1153) takes up the same question and reaches much the same conclusion as St. Gregory. In the monastic life, according to St. Bernard, there are three vocations: that of Lazarus the penitent; that of Martha, the active servant of the monastic household; and that of Mary, the contemplative. Mary's portion is the best of the three, and therefore she should never leave her contemplation unasked to share

in the labors of Martha. Yet the monastery needs adminis-
trators who will care for the temporal needs of the monks.
Martha's portion, therefore, should not be looked down
upon. Indeed, St. Bernard suggests that Mary and Martha
supplement one another. "After all, Mary and Martha are
sisters and they should dwell together in the same household in peace." In fact, for St. Bernard, true monastic perfection consists in "the union of all three vocations: that of
the penitent, the active worker (in the care of souls above
all) and the contemplative."*

---

*In *Thomas Merton on St. Bernard,* Merton developed in detail St. Bernard's understanding of the three vocations in the Cistercian life: "Commenting upon the
Gospel of the Feast [of the Assumption of the Blessed Virgin Mary], St. Bernard
compares the monastery to the family which Jesus used to visit at Bethany. In the
monastic community we find Lazarus, the penitent, Martha engaged in adminis-
tration, and Mary the contemplative. All these three are necessary to make the
monastery what it ought to be, not only materially, but above all spiritually. They
are the effect of the good order of charity in the monastery. It would be a
distortion and a caricature of monastic life to demand that a community consist
exclusively of one or the other of these 'orders.' It is a corruption of the Cistercian
ideal to insist that everyone confine himself exclusively to the vocation of Lazarus.
It is a further falsification of the Cistercian ideal when, in actual practice, the
house becomes a collection of querulous and somewhat excitable Marthas. Mary
has chosen the best part. And yet not even Mary has a monopoly on the Cistercian
ideal. The monastery is not expected to consist exclusively of Marys sitting at the
feet of Jesus. If St. Bernard makes this last qualification, it is certainly not because
he regretfully accepts it as inescapable. We are not to believe that the monastery
ought to be peopled entirely by Marys but that, since human nature is what it is,
we must be content to let two-thirds of the community live below the level of our
true vocation. This is by no means the case. It is *better* that the community should
live on these different levels, and all who live on their own level within the
community are in fact *fulfilling* the Cistercian ideal." (pp. 30–31)

"The Abbot of Clairvaux has shown us that the contemplative life is to be
sought and preferred to the active life, but that the 'mixed' life, composed of
action and contemplation together, is in a certain sense more necessary to the
Church than contemplation alone and therefore it has a higher dignity than the
life of pure or unmixed contemplation . . . A very high degree of Christian
perfection is necessary for the 'mixed' life, according to St. Bernard. He says that
the most perfect souls combine in themselves the vocations of Martha, Mary and
Lazarus. They excel at the same time in apostolic action, in contemplation and
in works of penance." (p. 106)

When the monasteries of the Middle Ages lost their fervor, the last observance that ceased to be carried out was the choral office. Hence, those who attempted to reform the monasteries in the Counter-Reformation period did not turn their attention to the liturgy, because, though the soul may have gone out of it, it was still functioning in fairly good order; rather, they turned their reforming zeal to the sphere of personal prayer and piety, drawing on the *Devotio Moderna,* * with its insistence on personal devotion to the humanity of Christ and on affective prayer. The subjective element of prayer was emphasized and given primacy of importance over "objective" liturgical worship. The conclusion eventually arrived at was that, if you really wanted to pray, you waited till the office was over. Then, "spontaneous and subjective prayer can be given free rein." This mentality has survived in monasteries and also among clergy bound to the recitation of the office. In this context it is worth recalling the (probably apocryphal) story of the three priests on a boat saying their office together. When a sudden storm arose, one of them said: "We had better stop saying the office and start praying." The story is not atypical of the unhealthy attitude that prevails when the subjective experience of the individual at prayer becomes the sole criterion for judging the value and validity of all forms of prayer. The contemporary liturgical movement—especially with the more recent emphasis on the contemplative dimension of liturgical prayer—has restored a much needed perspective to this all too narrow understanding of Christian prayer.

DOM AUGUSTINE BAKER. Merton concludes his brief history of personal prayer in the Benedictine tradition with a

---

*The *Devotio Moderna* was a revival of spirituality that originated in Holland in the fourteenth century. It stressed the inner life of the individual and the methodical practice of meditation.

short evaluation of the interesting and unusual "case" of Dom Augustine Baker (1575–1641), the English Benedictine who fought a lifelong battle to restore contemplation to the monastic life as the sole and only legitimate reason for its existence.* His stance represents a significant departure from the traditional teaching on action and contemplation as we have seen it expressed in the writings of St. Gregory the Great and St. Bernard of Clairvaux. Dom Augustine Baker saw action and contemplation as separated by a great gulf, with no possibility of bridging the gap between them. "For Dom Augustine both liturgy and meditation were on the wrong side of the gulf. The real prayer was simple contemplative introversion."

> He found himself in a lifelong conflict with those of his brethren for whom he coined the caustic and ambiguous expression "the active livers" . . . [He] goes so far as to say that the trouble with monasteries is that they are usually run by "active livers" who destroy the life of prayer by frustrating the lives of the contemplatives ("the internal livers").

His stance was extreme and one that can scarcely be expected to appeal to modern Benedictines, who have espoused with enthusiasm the cause of the liturgical movement. His overemphasis of one aspect of the monastic life to the exclusion of all else created a false problem.

> The true vocation of the monks of the Benedictine family is not to fight for contemplation against action, but to restore the ancient, harmonious and organic balance between the two. Both are necessary. Martha and Mary are sisters.

Santa Sophia, or Holy Wisdom, is a posthumous collection of his ascetical writings that expounds his teachings on the way of contemplation.

VIII

Zen and the Birds of Appetite
(with some reflections
on Merton's Asian journey)

One of the striking features of the last decade of Merton's life was his enthusiastic appropriation of Zen—first of its vocabulary (e.g., in *New Seeds of Contemplation*), and then of its experience (in *Zen and the Birds of Appetite*). Three decades earlier, in the late 1930's, influenced by Huxley's book *Ends and Means,* Merton had dabbled in Oriental texts, only to be baffled by them. The rather sweeping conclusion he drew, writing later in *The Seven Storey Mountain,* was that Oriental mysticism, while "not per se evil, was simply more or less useless."

BRAMACHARI. His attitude toward Eastern religions was affected, though not actually changed, by his contact with a Hindu monk, Bramachari, whom he met for the first time in 1938 at Grand Central Station in New York. In *The Seven Storey Mountain,* Merton describes this "shy little man, very happy, with a huge smile, all teeth, in the midst of his brown face. And on the top of his head was a yellow turban with Hindu prayers written all over it in red. And on his feet, sure enough: sneakers." Merton and this Eastern monk became good friends; indeed, on his Asian journey in 1968 he tried, though without success, to contact his Hindu friend in Calcutta. Bramachari seemed to sense from the beginning that his young friend was feeling his way toward some settled religious conviction and toward some kind of life centered in God. He made no attempt, however, to change the young Merton's attitude toward the religions of the East; instead, he said to him: "There are many beautiful mystical books written by the Christians. You should read St. Augustine's *Confessions* and *The Imitation of Christ.*" Merton later reflected on Bramachari's advice:

> Now that I look back on those days it seems to be very probable that one of the reasons why God had brought him all the way from India was that he might say just that. After all, it is rather ironical that I had turned, spontaneously, to the East in reading about mysticism, as if there were little or nothing in the Christian tradition . . . So now I was told that I ought to turn to the Christian tradition, to St. Augustine —and told by a Hindu monk!

Five months after his meeting with Bramachari, Merton was received into the Roman Catholic Church. Three years later, on December 10, 1941, he entered the Abbey of Gethsemani to become a Trappist monk. As a monk, he read deeply in the "many beautiful mystical books written by the Christians." He steeped himself in the writings of the Church Fathers, the Fathers of the Desert, the great Cistercian writers, the fourteenth- and sixteenth-century mystics. His reading—and writing—firmly established him in the apophatic tradition that stemmed from Gregory of Nyssa and Pseudo-Dionysius down to the Rhenish mystics of the fourteenth century and St. John of the Cross in the sixteenth century. Over and over again, as we have seen in earlier chapters, Merton describes the contemplative experience as one of "self-naughting," darkness and negation that is beyond verbalization, beyond rationalization. More and more, he attempts to describe the contemplative life— as in the preface to the revised edition of *Seeds of Contemplation* he said he would do—in terms of experience rather than in precise dogmatic statements.

This emphasis on experience beyond concepts and verbalization inevitably led Merton back to Eastern thought, and especially to Zen. When in 1966 he writes about Zen: "The whole aim of Zen is not to make foolproof statements about experience but to come to direct grips with reality without the mediation of logical verbalization," his words are something of a summary of what for so many years he had been saying about Christian contemplation.

DAISETZ T. SUZUKI. If it was a Hindu monk who encouraged Merton to study Christian mystical writing, it was a Japanese Zen master, the late Daisetz T. Suzuki, who gave him an insight into Zen that enabled him to become one of its most authentic interpreters to the Western world. Merton's admiration for Suzuki was profound. In *Zen and the Birds of Appetite* he calls the Japanese scholar a remarkable man who "contributed no little to the spiritual and intellectual revolution of our time" and who brought "the active leaven of Zen insight" "into the already bubbling ferment of Western thinking." "Speaking for myself," Merton wrote, "I can venture to say that in Dr. Suzuki Buddhism finally became for me completely comprehensible, whereas before it had been a very mysterious and confusing jumble of words, images, doctrines, legends, rituals, buildings and so forth."

Merton's contact with Dr. Suzuki was threefold: in his many works in English on Buddhism and Zen, in a written dialogue with him published in 1961, and in a face-to-face dialogue at Columbia University in 1964. Merton was much impressed with Suzuki's writings, which he considered "the most complete and authentic presentation of an Asian tradition and experience" available to English-speaking readers. "The uniqueness of Dr. Suzuki's work," he wrote, "lies in the directness with which an Asian thinker has been able to communicate his own experience of a profound and ancient tradition in a Western language."

The written dialogue between them grew out of a book which Merton published in 1959 entitled *The Wisdom of the Desert.* The book was a translation of selected "Sayings" of the Desert Fathers. In translating the *Verba Seniorum,* Merton had been struck by the fact that the "Words" of the Desert Fathers bore a remarkable resemblance to some of the stories told of the Japanese Zen masters. "There are countless Zen stories that almost exactly reproduce the *Verba Seniorum*—incidents which are obviously likely to occur whenever men seek and realize the same kind of poverty, solitude and emptiness."

Merton sent the text of his translation to Dr. Suzuki with the suggestion that they engage in a dialogue about the "wisdom" of the Desert Fathers and the Zen masters. Suzuki accepted the invitation, and the dialogue that resulted was published in 1961 and reprinted as Part Two of *Zen and the Birds of Appetite.*

Significantly, Suzuki chose as the common ground for this dialogue between East and West, not the ascetical and meditative practices of the Desert Spirituality, but what Merton calls "the most primitive and most archetypal fact of all Judaeo-Christian spirituality: the narrative of the Creation and Fall of man in the Book of Genesis."

Suzuki equates the original state before the fall with Innocence—the state of undifferentiated unity, above the distinction of good and evil, in which everything one does is good. The human person becomes morally "concerned,"

Suzuki states, only after he falls out of the state of Innocence into the state of Knowledge: the Knowledge of good and evil. Knowledge begets "moral" consciousness, for it "differentiates just from unjust, good from evil, right from wrong, foe from friend." Knowledge has a pair of discriminating eyes: it sees no longer unity but difference. Since it is not seeing what really is, Suzuki identifies it with Ignorance.

Human life must involve keeping Innocence (Wisdom, *Prajna*) and Knowledge (Ignorance) in proper balance—a difficult thing to do in a world where "the growth of Knowledge is everywhere encouraged in a thousand and one ways." The human task is to regain, or, better, to recognize that one already possesses in a hidden way that primitive-mindedness which in the Genesis story is symbolized by Innocence and in Zen by Emptiness. The mind must be emptied of all that pollutes it. And what pollutes the mind is the egocentric consciousness; namely, the Ignorance (Knowledge) that distinguishes good from evil, ego from non-ego. Once the mind realizes the truth of Emptiness (Innocence), then it knows that there is no self, no ego, no atman. Emptiness is a state of zero in which all good is performed and all evil is avoided. This is "zero," not as a mathematical symbol but as the infinite—the storehouse of all possible good or values. Zero, Suzuki says, equals infinity and infinity equals zero.

Suzuki finds a parallel to "Emptiness" in the writings of the Rhenish mystic, Master Eckhart, who speaks of the "most intimate poverty" whereby a person is emptied of things, creatures, himself, and even God. If a person leaves in himself a place for God to act, he is not yet truly empty. For God Himself must be the place where God acts.

> If God once found a person as poor as this [i.e., without even a place for God], He would take the responsibility of

His own action and would himself be the scene of action, for God is one who acts within Himself. It is here, in this poverty, that man regains the eternal being that once he was, now is and evermore shall be.

It is only in this "most intimate poverty" of total Self-lessness, Dr. Suzuki tells us, that "we find ourselves to be the ordinary Toms, Dicks and Harrys we had been all along." For the experience of "Emptiness" is not only metaphysical and ontological, it is existential and empirical too.

In his reply to Suzuki, called "The Recovery of Innocence," Merton writes that the Desert Fathers went into the desert to seek the "lost innocence, the emptiness and purity of heart which had belonged to Adam and Eve in Eden." The paradise they sought was not an outward one but a paradise within themselves in which they would recover that unity that had been shattered by the "knowledge of good and evil." Humanity, once a unity in Adam, but divided into a "multitude" by the fall, recovers unity, innocence, and purity in Christ the New Adam. The individual dies with Christ to his "old man," that is his exterior, egotistical self, and rises in Christ to the new man, "a selfless divine being, who is the one Christ, the same who is all in all."

Merton sees the difference between Christianity and Buddhism in the fact that "emptiness" for the Buddhist seems to be a complete negation of personality, whereas "purity of heart" for the Christian means a supreme and transcendent fulfillment of personality. The problem, as he sees it, is that Christian thought and Zen thought often appear at opposite poles which actually fail to represent their true positions. Thus, Christian thought tends all too often to identify personality with the illusory, exterior ego-self, which is by no means the true Christian person. Buddhist thought, on the other hand, appears to deny any positive value to personality, yet this is not in fact Buddhist practice. For, as Dr. Suzuki states: when one has become "absolutely naked," he finds himself to be the ordinary Tom, Dick, or Harry that he had been all along. The difference, in part at least, is one of language: the Zen language of "Emptiness" being more radical, austere, and ruthless, and the Christian language of "purity of heart" expressing itself more in metaphorical terms and concrete imagery, though always with the realization that one must penetrate the surface and reach the inner depths. In any case, Merton says:

> The "death of the old man" is not the destruction of personality, but the dissipation of an illusion, and the discovery of the new man is the realization of what was there all along, at least as a radical possibility, by reason of the fact that man is the image of God.

Merton believes that Suzuki's formula, zero = infinity, can be equated with the basic Christian intuition of divine mercy, which is grace "considered not as a reified substance given to us by God from without," but "precisely as emptiness, as freedom, as liberality, as gift." In Christian thought, emptiness and nakedness, because they are pure gift, equal fullness.

> But lest the idea of gift be interpreted in a divisive "dualistic" sense, let us remember that God is His own Gift and that the Gift of the Spirit is the gift of freedom and emptiness. His giving emerges from His Godhead, and as Ruysbroeck says, it is through the Spirit that we plunge back into the essential nakedness of the Godhead where "the depths themselves remain uncomprehended. This is the dark silence in which all lovers are lost."

The Merton–Suzuki dialogue is sometimes difficult to follow—and still more difficult to summarize—as each tries to use the language of the other to clarify his own tradition. The fact that, despite differences of vocabulary, they were able to communicate in depth is at once a sign of the unique ability of each of them to interpenetrate with the thoughts of the other and a model of what interreligious dialogue can accomplish when one tradition opens its eyes to the reality of another. The exchange was possible only because each had penetrated to the depths of his own tradition. The "Innocence" of Thomas Merton encountered the "emptiness" of Daisetz Suzuki and they found that in many respects they were in the same "place," or, if one prefers, the same "no-place."

Having met Suzuki in his works and in written dialogue, Merton had the pleasure of meeting him in person when the Japanese scholar made his last visit to the United States. On June 12, 1964, Merton received a letter from Dr. Suzuki's secretary, Miss Okamura, saying that he would be in New York City and that, while he definitely could not come to Gethsemani, he would be pleased to have Merton come to meet him in New York. The abbot gave permission for the trip and on June 15 Merton flew out of Louisville bound for New York City. He recalled the thrill he experienced when the hostess asked him his destination and he said "New York" and realized that he was "going home."

The Trappist monk and the Zen scholar had two long talks.* Suzuki had read several of Merton's books and commended him for what he had written on Zen. Merton left

---

*Appropriately, their visit took place at Columbia University, where Merton had studied, and in New York, where twenty-six years earlier, to the very month, he had met under such different circumstances with the Hindu monk, Bramachari.

the talks profoundly impressed at the deep understanding that existed between himself and this frail but alert scholar, then ninety-four years of age, whose writings he had read for so long a time.

> One had to meet this man in order fully to appreciate him. He seemed to me to embody all the indefinable qualities of the "Superior Man" of the ancient Asian, Taoist, Confucian and Buddhist traditions. Or, rather, in meeting him, one seemed to meet that "True Man of No Title" that Chuang Tzu and the Zen Masters speak of. And of course this is the man one really wants to meet. Who else is there? In meeting Dr. Suzuki and drinking a cup of tea with him, I felt I had met this one man. It was like finally arriving at one's own home.

Merton felt, too, that in meeting Suzuki he had come to understand Buddhism as never before, not because they had talked about abstract doctrinal matters (for they had not), but because he had come face to face with a man who lived what he had written about. "One cannot understand Buddhism," Merton wrote, "until one meets it in this existential manner, in a person in whom it is alive."

Merton's encounters with Dr. Suzuki bore fruit not only in his own life but in a series of articles written after the New York City visit that were published in various places and gathered together in Part One of *Zen and the Birds of Appetite.*

The first instinct of one who may have a superficial acquaintance with Zen is to study it as a religion. As a religion, it may be placed in the context of Chinese and Japanese history and seen as "a product of the meeting of speculative Indian Buddhism with practical Chinese Taoism." One may read books about Zen and make the assumption that, in doing so, he is learning the "doctrines" of Zen. He may then compare these with the doctrines of Christianity and perhaps reach the conclusion that, apart from the fact that both have something to do with meditation,* they are otherwise utterly alien to one another.

One could do this and perhaps find some justification in the history of religions for doing so; yet he would miss the point of Zen. For, whatever historical studies may have to say, responsible practitioners of Zen deny that it is a religion. They deny that it is a sect or school or that it is confined to Buddhism and its religious structure. "Zen is outside all structures and forms." It is not a world view or an ideology that attempts to explain the meaning of reality: indeed, Zen does not attempt to explain anything. It is not a philosophy: it refuses to make statements about the metaphysical structure of being and existence. It is not a theology: it is not concerned with God. It neither denies nor affirms a Supreme Being, though it is possible "to discover sophisticated analogies between the Zen experience of the Void (*Sunyata*) and the experience of God in the 'unknowing' of apophatic Christian mysticism." Zen is not a doctrine constructed to explain the Buddha's experience of enlightenment in order to propose it as a matter of "faith": rather, it seeks "an existential and empirical participation in that enlightenment experience."

Zen is consciousness that is trans-formed. As such, it is beyond any system, structure, or religion that would try to categorize or classify it. "But," says Merton, "it can shine through this or that system, religious or irreligious, just as light can shine through glass that is blue, or green, or red, or yellow. If Zen has any preference, it is for glass that is plain, has no color, and is 'just' glass."† This trans-formed

---

*The term "Zen" is the Japanese equivalent of Ch'an, which, in turn, is the Chinese equivalent of the Sanskrit word "dhyana," which means "meditation."
†Thus, Dom Aelred Graham has written a book called *Zen Catholicism*, and William Johnston one called *Christian Zen*.

consciousness or superconsciousness has been compared by a modern Zen writer to a mirror.

> The mirror is thoroughly egoless and mindless. If a flower comes it reflects a flower, if a bird comes it reflects a bird. It shows a beautiful object as beautiful, an ugly object as ugly. Everything is revealed as it is. There is no discriminating mind or self-consciousness on the part of the mirror. If something comes, the mirror reflects; if it disappears the mirror just lets it disappear.

The meaning is that Zen consciousness does not try to fit things into artificially conceived, a priori structures. It is simple attentiveness to reality. It "simply sees what is there and does not add any comments, any interpretation, any judgment, any conclusion. It just *sees.*" This freedom from categorizing and classifying is exemplified in Zen language, which seems at times an anti-language, and in Zen logic, which often appears to be a reversal of philosophical logic.

Zen does not have the habit of verbalization and rationalization, so common in the West, whereby we tend to falsify even our ordinary experiences. As Merton puts it:

> The convenient tools of language enable us to decide beforehand what we think things mean and tempt us all too easily to see things only in a way that fits our logical preconceptions and our verbal formulas.

We do not see things as they are; we manipulate them to fit our prejudices.

> Zen uses language against itself to blast out these preconceptions and to destroy the specious "reality" in our minds, so that we can *see directly.* Zen is saying, as Wittgenstein said: "Don't think: Look!"

Zen is interested in the real, not the verbal. "When I raise the hand thus, there is Zen," says Daisetz T. Suzuki. "But

when I assert I have raised the hand, Zen is no more there."
As soon as you conceptualize an experience, you objectify
it, and there is danger of confusing the concept with the
experience itself, of forgetting that what is described is not
what is real. "The whole aim of Zen," Merton tells us, "is
not to make foolproof statements about experience, but to
come to direct grips with reality without the mediation of
logical verbalizing."

The awareness of Zen, therefore, is not the self-conscious awareness of a reflecting, knowing, talking ego, but
pure awareness—an awareness that is immediately present
to itself. It is not the experience of an ego-subject; it is
experience pure and simple. "It just sees. Sees what? Not
an Absolute Object, but Absolute Seeing."

Zen is a direct experience of life, seized bare-handed,
with no gloves on (as Suzuki puts it), that is at once an
experience of undifferentiated unity and at the same time
of existential concreteness. It is not an abstract grasp of
pure being: not an idealism that lays hold of invisible realities that lie beyond the visible, of noumena that are above
phenomena. Rather, the invisible is grasped as imbedded
in the visible; the noumena, in the phenomena. *Nirvana* is
samsara. * Enlightenment, trans-formed consciousness, is to
be found in the realities of one's daily life, in the flow of life
with which one is identified. "There is certainly," Merton
says, "a kind of living and non-verbal dialectic in Zen between the ordinary everyday experience of the senses
(which is by no means arbitrarily repudiated) and the experience of enlightenment." Enlightenment is the attainment
of the "Buddha-mind," yet an attainment that is no attainment, for the "Buddha-mind" is not something esoteric

---

*In simplest terms, *nirvana* means the enlightenment experience, and *samsara*
means everyday existence.

that is "not there" which has to be put there. "The Buddha-
mind is your everyday mind." Hence, the Zen saying that
going to a monastery to seek enlightenment is like a man
riding on an ass in search of an ass.

Zen, therefore, is not, like Christianity, a revelation of
life's meaning (though Christianity, too, when properly understood, is more than that); rather, it is a direct grasp of
life in its unity and concreteness, in its pure, inarticulated
ground—a grasp of what was always there, but not perceived, because an ego-subject cannot perceive it.

> [Zen] does not bring news which the receiver does not
> already have, about something the one informed did not yet
> know. What Zen communicates is an awareness that is poten-
> tially already there but is not conscious of itself. Zen is, then,
> not Kerygma* but realization, not revelation but conscious-
> ness, not news from the Father Who sends His Son into this
> world, but awareness of the ontological ground of our own
> being here and now, right in the midst of the world.

Since Zen is a direct grasp of what was always there, right
in the midst of the world, it is perfectly logical to say with
Suzuki that "Zen teaches nothing": it merely enables one
to wake up and become aware. True wisdom *(Prajna)* is not
a replacement of old knowledge with new knowledge; it is
a transformation whereby one knows what was always po-
tentially knowable. Hence, the Zen master, when asked
"What is knowledge?" could answer: "It is no knowledge."
For, with enlightenment, nothing new is added from the
outside. Or, as the Zen saying puts it: "When enlighten-

Kerygma in the New Testament is the announcement of the good news that God
has saved us in Jesus Christ. But it should be remembered that the *Kerygma* does
not call us to be something we were at first not intended to be. It is rather a call
to *realize* what God from the beginning willed us to be. The *Kerygma* is the
announcement of the mystery hidden in God from all eternity: His will to make
all one with Him in Christ. See Ephesians 1:10.

ment is achieved, nothing is known, nothing is unknown." "Nothing is known," for no new knowledge has been acquired (it was already there). "Nothing is unknown," for the phenomenal world is simply a manifestation of "the primordial emptiness in which all things are one."

Merton believed that the modern person, so fragmented in his own life, so divided from other people, so caught up in his own prejudices that he lives more often with illusion than with reality, has much to learn from Zen. For "it is nondoctrinal, concrete, direct, existential, and seeks above all to come to grips with life itself, not with ideas about life."

CHRISTIANITY AND ZEN. Dom Aelred Graham's *Zen Catholicism* and William Johnston's *Christian Zen* suggest by their very titles the possibility of a dialogue between Christianity and Zen. Yet Merton, initially at least, seems to be dubious about such a possibility. He points out: "You can hardly set Christianity and Zen side by side and compare them. This would almost be like trying to compare mathematics and tennis." What he seems to be saying is that it would be better to treat each by itself, without attempting any rapprochement between them. Yet this is clearly not Merton's intent, for the obvious purpose of his dialogue with Suzuki, as also of the other chapters in *Zen and the Birds of Appetite,* is precisely to show the points of intersection between these two approaches to reality.

The point that Merton is intending to make is, I believe, that you cannot compare Christianity and Zen as religions; you cannot compare them at the level of doctrine. As he puts it: "To approach the subject [of Zen] with an intellectual or theological chip on the shoulder would end only in confusion." For Zen is neither an intellectual approach to reality nor a theological explanation of human existence. Christianity, on the other hand, seems at first sight to be both. Zen is realization; it is not doctrine. Christianity is revelation; and through the centuries that revelation has been formulated into an elaborate system of doctrinal statements. Christianity is verbal: much ink has been spilled in expounding its doctrines. Zen is, as far as possible, nonverbal. To compare the two at the level of doctrine, therefore, would be futile. For Christianity, doctrine is of primary importance; in Zen, it is accidental.

But there is a possible point of meeting for the two; namely, at the level of experience. Zen gives priority to experience; but so does Christianity, if it is properly understood. It is true that Christianity, unlike Zen, begins with revelation. But it is a mistake to think of this revelation simply as doctrine; it is the self-revelation of God calling the Christian to experience Him in Christ. Granted this revelation is communicated in words and statements, and Christians have always been profoundly concerned with the exact meaning of these statements and their precise formulation. Nonetheless, Christian theologians, at least in their better moments, have always understood that no conceptual formulation can adequately embody God's self-revelation. We must admit, however, the fact, to which history testifies all too well, that obsession with correct doctrinal formulas has often made people forget that the heart of Christianity "is *a living experience* of unity with Christ which far transcends all conceptual formulations."

This was the realization of the Apostolic Church. The *Kerygma* of the early Church was not simply an announcement of certain propositions about Jesus Christ dead and risen; it was a summons to participate in the reality of His death and rising. It was a call to taste and experience eternal life. "We announce to you the eternal life which was with the Father and has appeared to us. What we have seen and have heard we announce to you, in order that you also may have fellowship with us and that our fellowship may be with the Father and with His Son Jesus Christ."

> Too often the Catholic has imagined himself obliged to stop short at a mere correct and external belief expressed in good moral behavior, instead of entering fully into the life of hope and love consummated by union with the invisible God "in Christ and in the Spirit," thus fully sharing in the Divine Nature.

Christianity means much more than a change in behavior: it means a change in consciousness. And if it is understood in this way, it involves, just as truly as Zen, an experience that is trans-forming, an experience that can never be adequately grasped in verbal formulations.

It is worth noting that among the early Church Fathers theology was not so much reflection on doctrine as rather the experience of the realities that doctrines attempt to express. This is still true to a large extent in the Christian East, where the theologian is not thought of primarily as one who writes books or gives lectures on theology but as one who has had the experience of God. The theologian is the saint who has something to say about God because he has experienced Him.

With the rise of Scholasticism in the West, theology came more and more to be separated from experience, so that it has often become necessary to ask the question that Merton puts: ". . . To what extent does the theology of a theologian without experience claim to interpret correctly the 'experienced theology' of the mystic who is perhaps not able to articulate the meaning of his experience in a satisfactory way?"

The question is an important one, for Christianity is much more than the intellectual acceptance of a religious message by a blind faith that understands the message only in terms of the authoritative interpretations handed down by Church experts. "On the contrary, Faith is a door to the full inner life of the Church." It means "access not only to an authoritative teaching, but above all to a deep personal experience which is at once unique and yet shared by the whole Body of Christ, in the Spirit of Christ."

> [The] Holy Spirit is given to us in such a way that God knows Himself in us and this experience is utterly real, though it cannot be communicated in terms understandable to those who do not share it.

St. Paul calls this experience having "the mind of Christ."

> Now when we see that for Buddhism *Prajna* is describable as "having the Buddha-mind," we understand that there must surely be some possibility of finding an analogy somewhere between Buddhist and Christian experience.

Indeed, quoting the words of Eckhart: "In giving us His love God has given us the Holy Ghost so that we can love Him with the love wherewith He loves Himself," Suzuki calls them an exact expression of what Zen means by *Prajna*. Further, Merton points out, Suzuki also equates with *Prajna* Eckhart's words: "The eye wherein I see God is the same eye wherein God sees me."

It would seem clear that despite his initial reluctance to compare Christianity and Zen on theological grounds, Merton ultimately reaches the conclusion that theology may well be the most fruitful meeting place of Christian–Zen dialogue, so long as it is "theology experienced in Christian contemplation" and "not the speculative theology of textbooks and disputations."

Thomas Merton was much occupied with the problem of human consciousness: the need of a human person to arrive at an awareness of his true identity. The modern person, he believed, has open to him two approaches to consciousness. One begins with the thinking, self-aware subject; the other, with Being ontologically perceived as beyond and prior to any subject-object distinction. The first is the Cartesian reflexive awareness by which one is preoccupied with his ego-self and sees himself as a subject over against objects in the world; the second is a consciousness in which one transcends his ego-self and achieves an immediate experience of undifferentiated Being. The first involves a flight from being into verbalism and rationalization; the second, a discovery of the unity of being. The first has dominated Western thought since Descartes (1596–1650); the second is the approach to consciousness that is characteristic of the Zen perception of reality.

The Cartesian person is "a subject for whom his own self-awareness as a thinking, observing, measuring and estimating 'self' is absolutely primary." His stance in the world, Merton says, is characterized by self-consciousness, separateness, and spectatorship. His self-awareness involves no consciousness of unity with what is real but of separateness from it as other. With his self-awareness swirling about his own limited subjectivity, he gazes out upon a world of objects and other subjects without ever experiencing reality from within itself. He is man the "outsider." This Cartesian alienation from reality in a "solipsistic bubble" is well expressed in Rilke's verse:

> And we, spectators, always, everywhere,
> Looking at, *never out of,* everything!

For this Cartesian, thinking self, even God becomes an object that can be reached only by concepts. This perhaps is why an age that glorifies the ego-self is the age of "the death of God."

Cartesian thought began with an attempt to reach God as object by starting from the thinking self. But when God becomes object, he sooner or later dies, because God as object is ultimately unthinkable.

Indeed, Merton continues:

God as object is not only a mere abstract concept, but one which contains so many internal contradictions that it becomes entirely nonnegotiable except when it is hardened into an idol that is maintained in existence by a sheer act of the will.

Many Christians today, exhausted by the effort to preserve a contradiction in existence, "have let go the 'God-object' that their fathers and grandfathers still hoped to manipulate for their own needs."

Yet liberation from the strain of maintaining an "idol" in existence has not left the Cartesian consciousness any less imprisoned within itself. Hence, it feels the need to break out of itself and somehow to meet the "other" in "encounter," "openness," "fellowship," "communion." These are "in-words" for today's Cartesian person struggling in vain to escape his ego-prison. "I-Thou" relationships with the "other" have become the desirable goal. "Yet the great problem is that for the Cartesian consciousness, the 'other' too is object." Hence, it is legitimate to ask, as Merton does: "Is a genuine I-Thou relationship possible *at all* to a purely Cartesian subject?"

It is the bankruptcy of the Cartesian approach to reality that has led many people, including Merton, to seek another model for approaching reality. And many have found the Zen model a congenial one—a model that not only suits the needs of modern people but also squares well with the Christian contemplative experience of reality. Merton writes in *Conjectures of a Guilty Bystander:*

The taste for Zen in the West is in part a healthy reaction of people exasperated with the heritage of four centuries of Cartesianism: the reification of concepts, idolization of the reflexive consciousness, flight from being into verbalism, mathematics and rationalization. Descartes made a fetish out of the mirror in which the self finds itself. Zen shatters it.

Merton, therefore, reminds his readers that another model of consciousness—a metaphysical one—is available to a modern person. This model starts "not from the thinking and self-aware subject but from Being, ontologically seen to be beyond and prior to the subject-object division." Being is understood not as an object of empirical observation that a subject comes to know by a process of rationalization; rather, there is an immediate intuitive experience that goes beyond reflexive awareness. What is experienced is not an idea of being as something abstract and objective but rather a concrete non-objective intuition of what really is. It is not "consciousness of," but pure consciousness, "in which the subject as such 'disappears.' " The experience is, therefore, a unitive one in which the "other" is perceived not in separation but in oneness. It is a transcendent experience in which the ego-consciousness is left behind, so that the self is not its own center, around which all else orbits. Rather, "it is centered in God, the one center of all,* which is 'everywhere and nowhere,' in whom all are encountered and from whom all proceed. Thus, from the very start, this consciousness is disposed to encounter the 'other' with whom it is already united anyway 'in God.' "

To say that "the ego-consciousness is left behind" is not to deny the pragmatic psychological reality of the ego's self-awareness; it is simply to say that "once there has been

_____

*This center in which all are one would in Zen Buddhism be called the Void (*Sunyata*).

an inner illumination of pure reality, an awareness of the Divine, the empirical self is seen by comparison to be 'nothing.'" This is to say that "it is contingent, evanescent, relatively unreal, real only in its relation to its source and end in God, considered not as an object but as the free ontological source of one's own existence and subjectivity."

Such a transcendent experience liberates man from his inordinate self-consciousness and from his obsession with self-affirmation, "so that he may enjoy the freedom from concern that goes with being simply what he is and accepting things as they are." For in this experience one lets go of his own superficial thoughts and preoccupations that he may gain a deeper life in an unimpeded unself-conscious looking at reality. This deeper life is for the Christian a new and liberated life "in the Spirit." Zen calls it *Prajna*, which is "the mature grasp of the primordial emptiness in which all things are one."

It should be evident that, if the ego-consciousness is "left behind" in the transcendent experience, the empirical ego cannot be the subject of that experience. This forces a radical questioning of the whole nature of the experience precisely as experience. "Are we able to speak of 'consciousness' when the conscious subject is no longer able to be aware of itself as separate and unique?"

In attempting to answer this question, Merton returns to the personalist vocabulary that he used in *The Inner Experience* and in *New Seeds of Contemplation*. "The subject of this transcendent experience," he writes, "is not the ego as isolated and contingent, but the person as 'found' and 'actualized' in union with Christ. In other words, in Christian mysticism the identity of the mystic is never purely and simply the mere empirical ego—still less the neurotic and narcissistic self—but the 'person' who is identified with

Christ, one with Christ. 'I live now, not I, but Christ lives
in me' " (Galatians 2:20).

This "finding," "actualizing," which is an "awakening"
of the Transcendent Self or the Person, Merton describes
in different ways. In the preface to the Japanese edition of
The New Man, he calls it "spiritual rebirth."

> This deep consciousness to which we are initiated by
> spiritual rebirth is an awareness that we are not merely our
> everyday selves, but we are also one with One Who is beyond
> all human and individual self-limitation.

In *Zen and the Birds of Appetite* he calls it a participation in
"the mind of Christ." Quoting St. Paul's words to the Phi-
lippians: "Let this mind be in you which was also in Christ
Jesus . . . *who emptied himself* . . . obedient unto death . . .
Therefore God raised him and conferred upon him a name
above all names," Merton comments:

> This dynamic of emptying and of transcendence accu-
> rately defines the transformation of the Christian conscious-
> ness in Christ. It is a kenotic transformation, an emptying of
> all the contents of the ego-consciousness to become a void
> in which the light of God or the glory of God, the full radia-
> tion of the infinite reality of His Being and Love are manifes-
> ted.

As Eckhart expresses it with his characteristic directness:
"We love God with His own love; awareness of it deifies
us."

Similar to this kenotic experience of the Christian is the
Buddhist experience of *Sunyata.* The individual ego is completely emptied and takes on the mind of the Buddha.

> Thus the Buddhist enters into the self-emptying and en-
> lightenment of Buddha, as the Christian enters into the self-
> emptying (crucifixion) and glorification (resurrection and

ascension) of Christ. The chief difference between the two is that the former is existential and ontological, the latter is theological and personal.

But, Merton reminds us, when we speak of the Christian transformation of consciousness as being "personal," we must be careful to distinguish the person from the individual empirical ego.

What has been said of Christianity and Buddhism is actually true also in other higher religions: the path to transcendent realization is the path of self-emptying rather than self-fulfillment. The ego-self, instead of being realized in its limited selfhood, is described as simply vanishing out of the picture altogether. The reason for this seemingly negative terminology is "not that the person loses his metaphysical or even physical status, or regresses into non-identity, but rather that his real status is quite other than what appears empirically to us to be his status."

> Hence it becomes overwhelmingly important for us *to become detached from our everyday conception of ourselves as potential subjects for special and unique experiences, or as candidates for realization, attainment and fulfillment* . . . That is why a St. John of the Cross is so hostile to visions, ecstasies and all forms of "special experiences." That is why the Zen masters say: "If you meet the Buddha, kill him."*

Merton suggests that the difference between the "ego-self" and the "person" is a crucial area of dialogue between Eastern and Western religions. Is the transcendent consciousness achieved by the Buddhist the same as that

---

*William Johnston comments on this iconoclastic Zen statement. He suggests it means: if you see the Buddha, what you see is not the Buddha, so slay him! Johnston believes that a Christian, too, could say: "If you meet the Christ, slay him!"—the meaning being that what you see is not the Christ. See William Johnston, *Christian Zen* (Harper and Row, 1971), pp. 50–51.

achieved by the Christian? Do all religions meet "at the top," beyond their differing creeds and doctrines? Is having the Buddha-mind the same "experience" as having the mind of Christ? Merton believes that we have not yet learned enough about different states of consciousness and their implications to be able to answer these questions in a definitive way. They are, nonetheless, questions that must be discussed if there is to be fruitful ongoing dialogue between the East and the West.*

It was to further this dialogue that Merton journeyed to the East in 1968. (One cannot help but feel that after *Zen and the Birds of Appetite* this journey *had* to be the next step.) He went as a Christian monk, deeply grounded by years of study in his own tradition and totally committed to it, yet at the same time deeply convinced that there was much he could learn from firsthand experience of Eastern monasticism. In the notes he had prepared for a talk at the Temple of Understanding Conference† in Calcutta on October 23, 1968, he had written:

> I think we have now reached a stage of (long-overdue) religious maturity at which it may be possible for someone

---

*In an interesting letter written to Erich Fromm on February 7, 1966, Merton speaks of a conversation he had with Ivan Illich: "We had some discussions on the question of a non-theistic religious experience. The point I was trying to convey was that religious experience in the Jewish, Christian, Zen Buddhist, or in a general mystical human way, is an experience which may not be different as a human experience in the case of a theist or a nonbeliever. I am not denying the significance of various conceptual frames of reference, but I do believe that when it comes down to the phenomenon of the religious experience itself, the theological frame of reference is not as crucial as it may appear to be" (Unpublished letter, Thomas Merton Studies Center, Louisville, Ky.).

†The Temple of Understanding is a worldwide organization of religious leaders established to foster communication and understanding among the religions of the world. Established in 1960, it held its first Spiritual Summit Conference in Calcutta in October 1968. Merton was invited to participate in this conference.

to remain perfectly faithful to a Christian and Western monastic commitment and yet to learn in depth from, say, a Buddhist or Hindu discipline and experience. I believe that some of us need to do this in order to improve the quality of our own monastic life and even to help in the task of monastic renewal which has been undertaken within the Western Church.*

Some might question the optimism with which Merton approached the East–West dialogue and the hopes he had for its success. No one can question the enthusiasm with which he entered into the dialogue. In reading *The Asian Journal,* one is amazed at the untiring eagerness with which he recorded subtle and often esoteric Hindu and Buddhist texts in his notebooks† and at the ease with which he seemed to establish instant rapport with the Dalai Lama and the many other holy persons whom he met on his journey.

Even if it be conceded that he was overly optimistic about the possible fruits of East–West contemplative dialogue (a concession that one need by no means necessarily make), he was in no sense "naïve" about the "rules" that must guide the dialogue. He spelled them out most clearly in the notes he prepared for the Calcutta talk: (1) The dialogue must be reserved for those who have been seriously disciplined by years of silence and by a long habit of meditation. (2) It must avoid a facile syncretism, by (3) scrupulously respecting important differences that exist between religious traditions. (4) It must concentrate, not on secondary matters (such as institutional structure, monastic rules,

---

*In the talk he actually gave at the conference, Merton did not speak from his prepared notes.

†On October 22, 1968, he recorded in his journal: "I've had the idea of editing a collection of pieces by various Buddhists on meditation, etc., with an introduction of my own" (*Asian Journal,* p. 31).

and suchlike), but on what is essential to the monastic quest: namely, the meaning and experience of self-transcendence and enlightenment achieved through transformation of consciousness.*

Monastic dialogue between East and West, following such guidelines, was of crucial importance, Merton felt, for today's world. For the monk has something important to say to modern men and women, and he needs to say it with utmost clarity. Dialogue with other monastic traditions can help prepare him for the task.

> It is the peculiar office of the monk in the modern world to keep alive the contemplative experience and to keep the way open for modern technological man to recover the integrity of his inner depths.

But, ultimately, communication through dialogue is not enough. Communication with words must yield place to communion without words: communion which, while it cannot dissolve differences, can in a certain way surmount them. For "communication takes place between subject and object; but communion is beyond the division: it is a sharing in basic unity."† This is what Merton was talking

---

*These guidelines systematize what Merton had said earlier about religious dialogue: "I will be a better Catholic, not if I can *refute* every shade of Protestantism, but if I can affirm the truth in it and still go further. So too with the Muslims, the Hindus, the Buddhists, etc. This does not mean syncretism, indifferentism, the vapid and careless friendliness that accepts everything by thinking of nothing. There is much that one cannot 'affirm' and 'accept,' but first one must say 'yes' where one really can. If I affirm myself as a Catholic merely by denying all that is Muslim, Jewish, Protestant, Hindu, Buddhist, etc., in the end I will find that there is not much left for me to affirm as a Catholic: and certainly no breath of the Spirit with which to affirm it" (*Conjectures of a Guilty Bystander*, p. 144).

†Merton continues: "Christianity sees this unity as a special gift of God, a work of grace, which brings us to unity with God and one another in the Holy Spirit. The religions of Asia tend to see this unity in an ontological and natural principle

about when he concluded his Calcutta talk with these words:

> If [all] are faithful to their own calling . . . and to their own message from God, communication on the deepest level is possible.
> And the deepest level of communication is not communication, but communion. It is wordless. It is beyond words, and it is beyond speech, and it is beyond concept. Not that we discover a new unity. We discover an older unity. My dear brothers, we are already one. But we imagine that we are not. And what we have to recover is our original unity. What we have to be is what we are.

On November 16, 1968, Merton met Chatral Rimpoche, "the greatest rimpoche I have met so far," he said, "and a very impressive person."* They talked for two hours, discussing points of Christian and Buddhist doctrine: the Risen Christ, *dharmakaya*, † suffering, compassion for all creatures. Chatral told Merton that he had meditated in solitude for thirty years and had not attained to perfect emptiness; Merton agreed that he hadn't either.

> The unspoken or half-spoken message of the talk was our complete understanding of each other as people who were somehow on *the edge* of great realization and were trying, somehow or other, to go out and get lost in it.

---

in which all beings are metaphysically one. The experience of unity for the Christian is unity 'in the Holy Spirit.' For Asian religions it is unity in Absolute Being (Atman) or in the Void (Sunyata). The difference between the two approaches is the difference between an ontologist mysticism and a theological revelation: between a return to an Absolute Nature and surrender to a Divine Person."

*"Rimpoche," meaning "the precious one," is a name given to spiritual masters in Tibetan Buddhism.

†*Dharmakaya* means the cosmic body of the Buddha, or the Buddha as Absolute Reality.

Did that realization come to Merton on December 2, 1968, when he visited Polonnaruwa in Ceylon and saw the Buddha figures there—the huge seated Buddha beside a cave, and a reclining Buddha on the right, with Ananda standing at attention? He describes the experience:

> Looking at these figures, I was suddenly almost forcibly jerked clean out of the habitual, half-tied vision of things, and an inner clearness, clarity, as if exploding from the rocks themselves, became evident and obvious . . . I do not know when in my life I have ever had such a sense of beauty and spiritual validity running together in one aesthetic illumination . . . My Asian pilgrimage has come clear and purified itself. I mean, I know I have seen what I was obscurely looking for. I do not know what else remains, but I have now seen and have pierced through the surface and have got beyond the shadow and the disguise.

What was the "surface" he had pierced through? Was it that of Asia or of himself? Though the words seem to mean the first, they could also mean the second. Had Merton come halfway across the world to realize at last the experience of emptiness and that total transformation of consciousness that were the goal of his life? Had he, in the presence of the Buddha figures, at long last entered fully into the kenotic experience of the paschal mystery and put on the mind of Christ? We cannot answer these questions; and perhaps we have no right to ask them. But this much we can say: his conversation with Chatral Rimpoche and his experience at Polonnaruwa give a special poignancy to the words he spoke on the last day of his earthly existence. In Bangkok on December 10, 1968, he said to a gathering of Christian monks and nuns from various parts of Asia:

> The monk is a man who has attained or is about to attain, or seeks to attain, full realization. He dwells in the center of

society as one who has attained realization—he knows the score. Not that he has acquired unusual or esoteric information, but he has come to experience the ground of his own being in such a way that he knows the secret of liberation and can somehow or other communicate this to others . . .

The whole purpose of the monastic life is to teach men to live by love. The simple formula, which was so popular in the West, was the Augustinian formula of the translation of *cupiditas* into *caritas*, of self-centered love into an outgoing, other-centered love. In the process of this change the individual ego was seen to be illusory and dissolved itself, and in place of this self-centered ego came the Christian person, who was no longer just the individual but was Christ dwelling in each one.

These are words he might have spoken to the monks at Gethsemani. It is indeed a paradox of Divine Providence that this "pilgrim of the Absolute," who had insisted that his monastery was not a "home," spoke these words thousands of miles away from his monastery; and then, in solitude, joined the company of "the burnt men."

Conclusion

Naomi Burton Stone has said: "Each one of us knows a different Thomas Merton." Though she was speaking of those who knew him personally, what she said is true also of those whose only acquaintance with him is through his writings. Some know him in his poetry; others, in his social criticism. Some find in his writings the road to solitude; others, the road to the East. He was many things for many people; yet, for all that, he was not a divided man. Though he ranged wide in his interests and concerns, everything about him comes together in the unity of his monastic vocation.

Thomas Merton wrote as a monk. He saw the world through the eyes of a monk: the downcast eyes of his early flight from the world; the wide-open eyes of his later years that looked out upon the world with love and compassion. During the last years of his life, when he was much occupied with the study of other religious traditions—Zen, Sufism— he was with equal energy writing on the renewal of monastic life. And in 1968, when he journeyed to the East, his purpose was monastic: to meet with Western monks who lived in Asia and to experience Buddhist monasticism at first hand. When death came suddenly to him at Bangkok on that fateful day of December 10, 1968, it was at a gathering of monks. He died as he had lived: a monk among monks.*

A monk, as he said in *The Silent Life,* is a man whose whole life is devoted to the search for God. He is a man for whom God alone suffices. Living a desert existence on the margins of society gives him a vantage point from which he can take up a critical attitude toward the world, its structures, and the kind of values it treasures. That is why he leaves the world: not to abandon it, but to free himself from its delusions so that he can offer it a vision of hope rooted in faith and love. But before he can offer that vision he must have experienced it in his own life. That is why contemplation is so crucial to his very existence and to his mission for the sake of the world. He cannot probe the heart of the world unless he has first sounded the depths of his own inner truth.

This is not to say that one becomes a contemplative *in order* to offer a message to the world. The contemplative life is justified by its own intrinsic meaning; it needs no purpose

---

*The statement of Edward Rice that Merton was "an Englishman who became a Communist, then a Catholic, later a Trappist monk, and *finally a Buddhist*" (*The Man in the Sycamore Tree,* Doubleday, 1972, p. 187) totally misrepresents Merton. It is true that he said before leaving for his Asian trip: "I intend to become as good a Buddhist as I can" (see David Steindl-Rast, "Recollections of Thomas Merton's Last Days in the West," reprint from *Monastic Studies,* Pine City, N.Y., p. 10). Yet he said it in much the same way a layman might say: "I intend to become as good a monk as I can." When the writer asked Brother David about the import of Merton's statement, his reply was: "It was said laughingly, as were many of Merton's statements, especially the weighty ones. (There are things that are too serious for saying them with a serious face.)" (Letter to the writer, November 29, 1979).

outside itself to validate it. But because he is a contemplative, the monk has (or should have) something of deep significance to say to the world.

To say that the contemplative has a vision to share and a message to proclaim is not to say that he has a blueprint which, if accepted, would solve the problems that beset today's world. The contemplative is not a problem-solver but a prophet. He is the "troubler of Israel" who prods the consciences of people and directs their minds and hearts to the real issues of human existence. If he has achieved that purity of heart which is the fruit of contemplation, he is less likely to be taken in by the surface confusion that the world mistakes for reality. He is more likely to be committed to values that the world searches for, though not always knowingly: values that are permanent, deeply human, and truly spiritual.

On August 21, 1967, in response to a request from Pope Paul VI for a message of contemplatives to the world, Merton wrote a moving message to his brothers and sisters "in the world," which perhaps sums up the vision the contemplative has to offer to his fellow men and women. He talks about the questions that "torment the man of our time":

> I do not know if I have found answers. When I first became a monk, yes, I was more sure of "answers." But as I grow old in the monastic life and advance further into solitude, I become aware that I have only begun to seek the questions. And what are the questions? Can man make sense out of his existence? Can man honestly give his life meaning merely by adopting a certain set of explanations which pretend to tell him why the world began and where it will end, why there is evil and what is necessary for a good life? My brother, perhaps in my solitude I have become as it were an explorer for you, a searcher in realms which you are not able to visit —except perhaps in the company of your psychiatrist. I have

been summoned to explore a desert area of man's heart in which explanations no longer suffice, and in which one learns that only experience counts.

He speaks of hope: "It is my joy to tell you to hope though you think that for you of all men hope is impossible. Hope not because you think you can be good but because God loves us irrespective of our merits and whatever is good in us comes from His love, not from our doing." He concludes with a call to his contemporaries to enter into the solitude of their own hearts:

> The message of hope the contemplative offers you, then, brother, is not that you need to find your way through the jungle of language and problems that today surround God; but that, whether you understand or not, God loves you, is present to you, lives in you, dwells in you, calls you, saves you, and offers you an understanding and light which are like nothing you ever found in books or heard in sermons. The contemplative has nothing to tell you except to reassure you and say that if you dare to penetrate your own silence and dare to advance without fear into the solitude of your own heart, and risk the sharing of that solitude with the lonely other who seeks God through you and with you, then you will truly recover the light and the capacity to understand what is beyond words and beyond explanations because it is too close to be explained: it is the intimate union in the depths of your own heart, of God's spirit and your own secret inmost self, so that you and He are in all truth One Spirit. I love you in Christ.

The statement is powerful and moving; yet it must be said that it betrays the dichotomy, sometimes disconcerting, that so often surfaces in Merton's writings on contemplation. He speaks as a contemplative about contemplation; but his message is for noncontemplatives. Merton seems never to have quite abandoned the "elitist" view of contemplation that for all practical purposes restricted it to the monastic life.* It is not that he thought that monks were superior people or that they loved God more than those who were not monks. It is simply that he believed that "life in the world" does not provide the atmosphere in which contemplation can flower. Yet he was not entirely consistent, for in book after book, written for a general readership, he invites his readers to enter into the contemplative experience. Was he perhaps saying that there is a difference between being a contemplative (the very condition of which involves withdrawal from the everyday affairs of life) and having a contemplative dimension in one's life, which is not only possible but essential for anyone who wants to live his life with some degree of depth and wholeness? Whether this represents his position or not, it is the writer's conviction that thousands of readers interpreted him in this way and have "translated" what he says about "monastic" contemplation into terms more congenial to their own way of life.

But perhaps the issue needs to be pressed further. Is there really a distinction between "being a contemplative" and "having a contemplative dimension in one's life"? Much depends on the way one views existence in the world. Does that existence involve a dichotomy between the supernatural and the natural, the sacred and the secular? Is the monk's life "contemplative" because habitually he moves in the order of the supernatural and the sacred? And can the lay person at best have only a "contemplative dimension" to his life, because most of that life involves engagement in the natural and the secular?

---

*Merton's position on "who can be a contemplative" is not always clear. See above, pp. 30–32; 37. See also pp. 208–12 on the "subject" of the transcendent experience.

Grappling with this dichotomy—supernatural vs. natural, sacred vs. secular—is not peculiar to Merton. It is a problem that has a long history. One confronts it in almost all mystical literature. Indeed, it is a particular way of stating a more general problem that has engaged philosophers and theologians for centuries: Is reality One or Many? Do we view reality in terms of dualism or nondualism?

This is the unspoken question beneath much of what Merton wrote about contemplation. And, because of his preference for the apophatic way, the thrust of his answer is always (though not without ambiguity)* in the direction of nondualism. Consistently, he presents the contemplative experience as a unitive one. In contemplation, one rises above the duality of subject and object: the subjectivity of the contemplative becomes one with the subjectivity of God. In contemplation, I, as a separate ego, vanish out of the picture and there is only God. In so early a book as *Seeds of Contemplation,* he had written: "Where contemplation becomes what it is really meant to be, it is no longer something poured out of God into a created subject, so much as God living in God and identifying a created life with His own Life so that there is nothing left of any significance but God living in God."† Yet, in *New Seeds of Contemplation,* written twelve years later, Merton speaks of our true reality

---

*Yet it should be remembered that in his writing Merton had always to keep in mind the censors (or, as they were later called, the "readers") who would review what he had written with an eye to its "Catholic orthodoxy."

†In *Christian Zen* (p. 22), Johnston quotes a letter he received from Merton in which he refers to a somewhat startling nondualistic statement of Eckhart. The Rhenish mystic speaks of a man so poor that he has not even a place for God. It is as if he is saying: God vanishes and only Eckhart remains, not Eckhart in his separate ego, but Eckhart as the person inseparable from God and one with Him. In other words it is THE ONE who remains, not Eckhart as a separate individual, not "God" as an "object," but only THE ONE. No wonder the scholastic theologians did not know quite what to make of Eckhart!

as being "in God" and "with Him," yet he feels constrained (perhaps by his scholastic training?) to add: "Of course [this reality] is ontologically distinct from Him."

It would seem that the nondualism implicit, but not unambiguous, in his earlier writings finally becomes explicit in *Zen and the Birds of Appetite.* His discussion in that book of the "subject" of the transcendent experience makes sense only in the framework of nondualism. If his preference for the apophatic way moved him toward nondualism, it was his exposure to Zen that pushed him to take the final step in that direction.

Yet Merton was a practical man. He knew that life presents us with dualities and that we have to live with them until we are able to surmount them. Brother David Steindl-Rast records an interesting conversation with him at Our Lady of the Redwoods Abbey in Whitethorn, California, just before he left for his Asian journey. Merton was speaking about the prayer of intercession: "We are not rainmakers, but Christians. In our dealings with God he is free and so are we. It is simply a need for me to express my love by praying for my friends; it is like embracing them. If you love another person, it is God's love being realized. One and the same love is reaching your friend through you, and you through your friend."

When Brother David asked him, "But isn't there still an implicit dualism in all this?" Merton answered: "Really there isn't, and yet there is. You have to see your will and God's will dualistically for a long time. You have to experience duality for a long time until you see it's not there. In this respect I am a Hindu. Ramakrishna has the solution. Don't consider dualistic prayer on a lower level. The lower is higher. There are no levels. Any moment you can break through to the underlying unity which is God's gift in Christ. In the end, Praise praises. Thanksgiving gives thanks. Jesus prays. Openness is all."

"You have to experience duality for a long time until you see it's not there." These words have the ring of autobiography. What counts ultimately is not what you say or think but what you experience. No one understood this better than Merton.* He wrote a great deal and (for a monk!) talked a great deal. But no one knew better than he that Life is not a matter of concepts or of words. It is not a question of talking yourself out of duality or reasoning your way to nonduality. Life is opening yourself to experience—first to this experience and that; and finally to Experience Itself.

It was because Merton was attuned to experience that he was preeminently a theologian—a contemplative rather than a dogmatic theologian. His theology was not an expounding of the truths of revelation in order to offer an intellectual appreciation of them; rather, it was the theology of one who could talk about God because he had first walked with God. For him, God was the burning mystery of Reality. God was the Great Experience beyond all experiences. No one in the twentieth century has articulated that Experience with such clarity of vision as Thomas Merton. Clifford Stevens intended no exaggeration when he wrote: "The men of the twenty-fifth and fiftieth centuries, when they read the spiritual literature of the twentieth century, will judge the age by Merton."

---

*See above: "I have been summoned to explore a desert area of man's heart in which explanations no longer suffice, and in which one learns that *only experience counts.*"

Works Cited

WORKS BY THOMAS MERTON

The Seven Storey Mountain. Harcourt Brace, 1948.
What Is Contemplation. St. Mary's, 1948; Burns Oates, 1950; Templegate, 1951, 1960, 1978.
Seeds of Contemplation. New Directions, 1949; revised edition, December 1949.
The Ascent to Truth. Harcourt Brace, 1951.
The Sign of Jonas. Harcourt Brace, 1953.
Bread in the Wilderness. Liturgical Press, 1953.
The Silent Life. Farrar Straus Giroux, 1957.
The Secular Journal of Thomas Merton. Farrar Straus Giroux, 1959.
The Inner Experience. 1959, unpublished (four drafts at Thomas Merton Studies Center, Louisville, Ky.).
The Wisdom of the Desert. New Directions, 1960.
The New Man. Farrar Straus Giroux, 1961.
New Seeds of Contemplation. New Directions, 1962.
Seeds of Destruction. Farrar Straus Giroux, 1964.
Mystics and Zen Masters. Farrar Straus Giroux, 1967.
Conjectures of a Guilty Bystander. Doubleday, 1966.
Zen and the Birds of Appetite. New Directions, 1968.

The Climate of Monastic Prayer. Cistercian Publications, 1969; also published as *Contemplative Prayer,* Herder and Herder, 1969.

The Asian Journal of Thomas Merton. New Directions, 1973.

Contemplation in a World of Action. Doubleday, 1973.

The Collected Poems of Thomas Merton. New Directions, 1977.

The Monastic Journey. Sheed Andrews McMeel, 1977.

Love and Living. Farrar Straus Giroux, 1979.

Thomas Merton on St. Bernard. Cistercian Studies Series, No. 9. Cistercian Publications, 1980.

OTHER WORKS

Aldhelm Cameron-Brown, "Seeking the Rhinoceros: A Tribute to Thomas Merton," *Monastic Studies,* 1969.

Aelred Graham, *Zen Catholicism.* Harcourt Brace, 1963.

Donald Grayston, "The Making of a Spiritual Classic: Thomas Merton's *Seeds of Contemplation* and *New Seeds of Contemplation,*" *Sciences Religieuses/Studies in Religion* 3 (1973–1974).

———, "Nova in Novibus: the New Material in Thomas Merton's *New Seeds of Contemplation,*" *Cistercian Studies* 10, 3 and 4 (1975).

Patrick Hart, ed., *Thomas Merton Monk.* Sheed and Ward, 1974.

William Johnston, *Christian Zen.* Harper and Row, 1971.

Sören Kierkegaard (Walter Lowrie, tr.), *The Concept of Dread.* Princeton, 1967.

Jacques Maritain, *Scholasticism and Politics.* Geoffrey Bles, 1945.

E. Allison Peers, ed., *The Complete Works of St. John of the Cross.* Burns Oates, vols. 1 and 2 (1934); vol. 3 (1935).

William H. Shannon, "Merton and the Discovery of the Real Self," *Cistercian Studies* 13, 4 (1978): 298–308.

David Steindl-Rast, "Recollections of Thomas Merton's Last Days in the West," *Monastic Studies* reprint.

Clifford Stevens, "Thomas Merton 1968: A Profile in Memoriam," *American Benedictine Review,* March 1969.

John F. Teahan, "A Dark and Empty Way: Thomas Merton and the Apophatic Tradition," *Journal of Religion* 58 (July 1978).

Evelyn Underhill, *Mysticism.* New American Library, 1955 (1910).

Notes

INTRODUCTION

I: WHAT IS CONTEMPLATION

[Unless otherwise noted, references are to *What Is Contemplation,* Templegate edition, 1978]

33   "the power" 50
33   "the ray" 41
33   "The darkness remains" 51

II: SEEDS OF CONTEMPLATION

[Unless otherwise noted, references are to *Seeds of Contemplation*]

34   "The seeds of this perfect life" *What Is Contemplation,* 16–17
35   "a collection of notes" 13
35   "The poet enters into himself" 71
35   "We are like vessels" 178
35   "By receiving His will" 19
36   "utterly transcends" 176
36   "above our natural capacity" 187
36   "the only reason" 176
36   "Contemplation by which we know" 144
36   "the fulfillment" 144
36   "All those who reach" 144
36   "Many are also destined" 144
37   "[The book] has no other end" 15
37   "The great majority of Christians" *What Is Contemplation,* 33
38   "There exists some point" 31
39   "lives in me" 33
39   "We become contemplatives" 33
39   "it strikes us" 144
39   "Although we had an entirely different notion" 144
39   "We enter into a region" 145
39   "the only way I can be myself" 29
40   "Since God alone possesses" 26
40   "the secret of who I am" 33
40   "discover who I am" 46
40   "shadowed by an illusory person" 46
40   "the illusion that is opposed" 34
41   "the fundamental reality of life" 28
41   "I am hollow" 29
41   "[my] life becomes a series" 33–34
42   "draw all the powers of my soul" 37
42   "God identifies" 196
42   "I must look for my identity" 41
42   "The more I become identified" 47
42   "merely because you happen" 57

III: THE ASCENT TO TRUTH

[Unless otherwise noted, references are to *The Ascent to Truth*]

IV: *THE INNER EXPERIENCE:* AN OVERVIEW

[Unless otherwise noted, references are to the fourth draft of *The Inner Experience*]

VI: NEW SEEDS OF CONTEMPLATION

[Unless otherwise noted, references are to New Seeds of Contemplation]

144   "In the twelve years" xiv
144   "contain a line" *Seeds,* 14
144   "We sincerely hope" xiv
144   "The author is talking" *Seeds* (rev. ed.), xii
145   "the man who spurned" *Contemplation in a World of Action* 159
146   "learn to share" 77
146   "a citadel" *Seeds,* 147; rev. ed., 142
146   "a wide impregnable country" 228
146   "Both are images" Grayston, "The Making of a Spiritual
       Classic," 353
146   "Contemplation is out of the question" 77
147   "Do not read" *Seeds,* 60
147   "Do not read" *Seeds* (rev. ed.), 46
147   "Do not read" 84
147   "More than twelve years" ix–x
149   "For the contemplative" 9
149   "the tragic anguish" 12
149   "We must remember" 7
149   "supremely personalistic" 153
150   "It is impossible" x
150   "cannot be clearly explained" 6
150   "It can only be hinted" 6
150   "the more he empties it" 6
150   "This reflection" 6–7
150   "life itself" 1
150   "A suspicion" Cameron-Brown, "Seeking the Rhinoceros,"
       68
151   "The author of this book" Preface to the Japanese ed. of
       Seeds of Contemplation, 1965 (unpublished ms.), 4
152   "his inveterate tendency" Grayston, "Nova in Novibus,"
       196
152   "Contemplation is the highest expression" 1
153   "Only the mystic" Underhill, *Mysticism,* 63
153   "spontaneous awe" 1
153   "gratitude for life" 1
153   breakthrough 6
153   vivid awareness 1
153   "awakening to the Real" 3
153   "Contemplation is the experience" 2
153   "loses its separate voice" 3
153   "Contemplation is the awareness" 5
154   "poor in concepts" 5
154   "too deep to be grasped" 1–2
154   "For contemplation is always" 2

VII: *THE CLIMATE OF MONASTIC PRAYER*

[Unless otherwise noted, references are to *The Climate of Monastic Prayer*]

VIII: ZEN AND THE BIRDS OF APPETITE

[Unless otherwise noted, references are to *Zen and the Birds of Appetite*]

242 / Notes

CONCLUSION

A Selective Index